FIENDS FELL

FLOOD EDITIONS, CHICAGO

TOM PICKARD
FIENDS FELL

Copyright © 2017 by Tom Pickard

All rights reserved

Published by Flood Editions

www.floodeditions.com

ISBN 978-0-9981695-2-1

Design and composition by Quemadura

Cover photograph by Tom Pickard

Printed on acid-free, recycled paper

in the United States of America

Thanks to the editors of *Chicago Review*,
Edinburgh Review, *Friday Night Boys*, *London
Review of Books*, *New Walk*, *Poetry*, *The Recluse*,
Starting at Zero, and Woodland Pattern Book Center for
publishing versions of this work. Some of it appeared in
Winter Migrants (Manchester: Carcanet Press, 2015).

FIENDS FELL JOURNALS

3

LARK & MERLIN

191

FOR GILL

As I walked up John Street thinking of you
I saw a slash of sea between houses

and felt, as always, no matter mood,
its or mine, something before thought

as though it were the source of language
and language the source of itself.

FIENDS FELL JOURNALS

O MY DEAR DEAR FRIEND! THAT YOU WERE
WITH ME BY THE FIRESIDE OF MY STUDY HERE,
THAT I MIGHT TALK IT OVER WITH YOU TO THE
TUNE OF THIS NIGHT WIND THAT PIPES ITS
THIN DOLEFUL CLIMBING SINKING NOTES ...

Samuel Taylor Coleridge

At the age of seventy Basil Bunting's second marriage disintegrated and he fled to the depths of Northumberland to occupy a winter-let that was damp and cold. He was my friend and mentor. At the age of fifty-six my own marriage has ended and I find myself situated on an escarpment along a stretch of the North Pennine Hills, two thousand feet above sea-level—exiled from my recent life and home by the South Tyne River which runs past its door. A river that could suddenly change after a storm from a sauntering lilting lyricism to a dangerous and ferocious force tearing trees out by their roots and washing away banksides. And it bled the colour of peat, dark and dangerous.

One day while it was high and raging I began to think of the forty or so houses, flats and squats that I'd lived in and felt for the first time that here was a place I could settle and grow old. In a book of poems, I wrote in 'a note on the author' *Tom Pickard lives by the South Tyne River, in the North Pennine Hills on the English–Scottish Border*. It placed me so precisely that it must have angered the god of drifter poets. Although the river is beyond hearing, when I look down into its valley from Fiends Fell where I am located I can see light reflected off its stealthy tributary, the Black Burn. The ridge overlooks Alston Moor on one side, and it is the most exposed part of that turbulent terrain, formerly famous for its lead and other minerals. William Hutchinson, the eighteenth-century historian, described it 'so wild a spot as Alston Moor; where all that the earth produces is from its bowels, and where the people also are so generally subterraneous.' And the subterranean reputation of the population was deepened one stormy day in the nineteenth century when after a wedding the bride and bridegroom decided to take a short cut home through the mines. They were never seen again, and under these hills there is a wandering couple waiting to come home.

Lead mining goes back at least as far as the Romans, and some of the imperial gutters and drains running with blood and wine originated here in the raw galena, rich in silver that was mined by slaves and prisoners and transported along The Maiden Way, a Roman road between Kirkby Thore, near Appleby, and Hadrian's Wall. The road cuts across the hazardously exposed fells, and traces can occasionally be seen beneath the heather.

The ridge forms the watershed and headwaters for three rivers that run into the North Sea some sixty miles away: the Tyne, the Wear and the Tees. On the west side water seeps in springs from the boggy earth covered in sphagnum moss and heather and rushes into tight precipitous cloughs to become tributaries of the

4

River Eden. The escarpment falls steeply into the valley of Eden and across to the mountains of the Lake District and sometimes when the sun is angled appropriately one of the lakes is visible and I can see where Coleridge and Wordsworth walked. Or if I look to the north, across the Solway Firth some fifty miles away, I can see hills that Burns, Hogg and Walter Scott would have known—and where part of *The Dream of the Rood*, possibly by Cædmon, is carved in runes on the eighth-century Ruthwell Cross.

The accommodation here is above and adjoining a café very popular with bikers and known to them as the Cardboard Café because several years ago it blew away overnight without leaving a trace—such is the strength of the winds on Fiends Fell. One in particular, called the Helm Wind, I await with nervous excitement. It is specific to this ridge and is spawned here and always blows at a force nine gale. The most recent howled at 130 miles per hour and the farmers in the Eden valley, immediately below the escarpment, say it rips turnips out of the ground, and an old woman claims that it blows the beaks off geese. Ruskin described it as one of the plague winds of the world and it is sometimes known as the Black Helm when it makes vegetation wither. But even the minor winds feel fierce enough to rip the holes from your socks and they make my bed shake. The draughts that icily burn through gaps in the wall and under tiles have blown paint, albeit already flaking, from the walls.

My bedroom is an attic, part of the gable end, and has two Velux windows facing east and west on the low slopes of the ceiling. The slate roof concerns me, as houses in this district are traditionally roofed with stone slabs six inches thick. It's where two weather systems meet and where, I'm told, winds blow from opposite directions at the same time, thus creating a kind of vortex; which prompted a friend to ask, what's it like living inside a metaphor?

PROLOGUE

when my lover became my enemy
I made a bed amongst winds
and drove the old road
till my heart crashed

where's the bypass?

1ST JUNE

At this height above sea-level, may blossom arrives late—and then only below the wind line on squat trees in tight cloughs.

The rain was stotting but I wanted to take pictures of the hawthorn in bloom and to inhale the scent, so I drove down into the South Tyne Valley to a tree that I had grown to know.

> *there is a hawthorn on a hill*
> *there is a hawthorn growing*
> *it set its roots against the wind*
> *the worrying wind that's blowing*
> *its berries are red its blossom so white*
> *I thought that it was snowing . . .*

Three hares scattered as I approached the lightning-divided trunk, like a couple in a lethally ecstatic dance.

MIDSUMMER

a blood-coloured star above
the swell of a reclining woman
backlit by sun sunk
behind skunk hills at midnight

16TH AUGUST

When I woke this morning I was groggy after working for eight hours in the café's take-away hatch selling drinks, sandwiches, burgers, bacon buns and a range of cakes to a continuous queue of hungry and thirsty bikers, cyclists and cars full of families. The hatch is barely more than a cupboard—a small cramped place in an annexe off the kitchen and facing the entrance. Vending from there, meeting demand en route, slightly eases the pressure on the women working inside the café.

And work is fast in the kitchen. Cauldrons of hot soup, large pans of steaming water, a vat of bubbling chip fat, one oven baking bread and cakes and another roasting meat. A whirl of pan stirring, dealing out portions, filling orders, peeling, chopping vegetables and fruit, dish washing, ploughing dough, slapping pastry, whisking, whipping eggs, cutting and slicing—all sidestepped by waitresses bringing and collecting orders. Generations work in the café, grannies, mothers, daughters—some from the Alston Moor side of the escarpment and others from villages below tucked in amongst the East Fells and directly in the path of the Helm Wind. These are its children and they can be as fast and furious. Jackie, who is responsible for keeping my hatch display supplied, shouts above the busy kitchen: 'Tom, do you need more muffin?'

'Only as much as I can get.'

When it closed I washed dishes and cleaned up, then ate dinner in the empty café at a table next to the French windows. During my meal a thunderstorm travelled over and on to the hills of Dumfries. Now the sky is clear and the air crisp, the sun is low over the Solway Firth, some fifty miles away—and I'm drunk with it.

READING CREELEY'S 'HISTOIRE DE FLORIDA'

Sightseers in a lay-by seek discernible facts
from a dissembling landscape,

like midday sun on the fleece of sheep
that lie and watch them drink
from polystyrene cups
filled from flasks, and photograph.

Banks of cloud stack up and pass.
A low owl blows in, easy as a breath of thistle.

The moon struck
a set of headlights over the hill and in my face.

The dead don't remember us.

21ST AUGUST

I took a walk to Black Fell and watched two buzzards and a family of kestrels riding the updraught with complete ease, for hours, to the sound of wind through stone walls and stiff rushes. Sky and mood and light change frequently.

There's been tension in the café kitchen and luminous pink cut-out stars with bold writing, saying things like 'no snapping', have been taped to the walls. Jayne Ann gave me a bowl of spicy veg soup so I wrote them a wee kitchen poem.

TODAY'S SPECIAL: SNAP SOUP

There's bitchin in the kitchen
bitchin in the kitchen
if it don't stop
lips will need stitching

Things were getting nasty
slapping that pasty
slapping that pasty

The roak came doon
and splattered the hill

They were saying nowt
but looks can kill

They were saying nowt
but slapping that pasty
Things were getting roaky
snappy and nasty

The cloud got dark
and the hill got misty
fat burnt me finga
and am feelin twisty

26TH AUGUST

Bob called saying he'd been over to Seaham in Co. Durham to Bill Griffiths' house to build him a computer. It was difficult to move in the front room of the small red-brick house, formerly part of a terrace of miner's cottages, because Bill had installed back to back two grand pianos on which he regularly played. He offered Bob a drink by throwing a teabag into a cup of cold water and putting it into a microwave oven.

Young guys kept walking in with local words for Bill, who was compiling one of his excellent dialect dictionaries. Bob said he's like fucking Fagin sending out pickpockets; only Bill's a word fence.

29TH AUGUST

Yesterday when I took my car into the garage at Alston, Ian Henderson talked about the weather being 'rowky'; it's Old Scots as well as Northern dialect for fog. A new one for me, 'nither' for shiver. His assistant, Jennifer, asked 'what's a cunny?' 'Any kind of culvert', he explained, although I suspect we all knew its cute anatomical association too. On the way home I plodged through a gushing cunny.

30TH AUGUST

Another fast wet foggy day. The night before last I slept with a window open and woke in the middle of the night to discover the duvet soaked through to the mattress. It wasn't raining when I went to bed, otherwise I would have covered it with a sheet of plastic that I normally use in wet weather, like an old dosser. I was too tired to get up and change the bedding so wriggled around until I could find a dry piece of mattress and duvet and went back to sleep.

A near-full moon must have been hovering above because the thick roak glowed.

I am ambivalent about the coming winter and find myself nervously pottering and preparing the workspace both physical and psychological. Tomorrow I will try to record wind on the fells as it will get my body moving and loosen up my thinking—gathering fuel for the winter.

2ND SEPTEMBER

My five-year-old grandson, Ottis, is staying here for a few more days. It's been a surprise to find how easy it is to have him around. I was thinking that his complications are not so difficult to resolve as those of his uncles but really they may be more complex. The dialogue between us, skipping the uncertainty of overlapping generations, is open and free of boundaries, and there is a calm comfortable respect for each other. But these thoughts are new and need time to grow.

A glass of wine and a homesick meadow pipit calls on a fence that fields the fell. When a curlew swallows a whirlpool of song Ottis, calling himself *Samurai-Jack*, leaps from a tabletop flapping his arms, showing how a swan takes off.

When I moved here three months ago I was both in awe of the wild and spooked by it and slept with a log-splitter under the bed to expel boarders, so I can understand Ottis's fear of sleeping alone in such a remote location.

As he sleeps on a mattress next to my bed I can hear his regular breath and a welcoming gentle westerly, like an affectionate bear growling at the window.

I think I'll stay here another year.

a silver-thin sunset dusted gold
obscures the valley

backlit larches
on a pencil line of distant hills

the slow mist's opaque drift

5TH SEPTEMBER

I recorded whistling winds from my window and caught an occasional clatter of dishes from the kitchen and the blown-about voices of the lasses.

Working in the café last Saturday I began to take a dislike to a couple of cyclists and felt like shouting, instead of their order number, 'burnt bacon butties for the bastards in blue Lycra'.

7TH SEPTEMBER

FIENDS FELL

It was a sun-bright day with a furious south-easterly as I lay sheltered from the blast in a deep body-sized dip of heather amongst fine grass and wild thyme to watch a kestrel drift into the wind above my skyline, about ten metres away. A small group of meadow pipits that habituate this summit became silent and lay low as it hovered close, hunting anything easy or careless. After a while the hawk was flipped off-kilter by a pair of ravens coming up from behind, shouldering the wind. Although struggling where the wind was fiercest they chose to get close to the hawk and forced it to flip and shift and drift to a patch of air three or four metres directly above where I lay and for a few long heart-hovering moments provided me the prey's point of view. When I moved the camera to my eye the hawk flipped back to its previous position. The ravens, meanwhile, had progressed only a short distance into the charging gale; although still strategically placed on either side of the kestrel they were unable to outmanoeuvre the wind with the same easy agility and resorted to barking, chastising or mocking the hawk—or so it seemed. The disturbance must have alerted any potential prey, so the raptor drifted out of sight. As I was reflecting on the incident and making a note it reappeared even closer than before and resumed hovering, but when a warplane burned in under the radar, hugging the contours, the bird flipped and surfed out of sight. Two other jets followed in a mock battle just as the ravens and hawk had done earlier.

BOOGIE–WOOGIE

how seamlessly boogie-woogie
becomes rock and roll

crows and gulls
airborne in a north-easterly

pass over the pass
'al reet, then'

her back to the blast
her wool hood up

crows skitter

all those years
keeping a low profile

it wasn't difficult

13TH SEPTEMBER

Flech; that's the word. I don't know where it came from, only it was the word I needed and would be the word I'd use. Dragged out of need I thought it an invention because I couldn't find it in my 'conscious' vocabulary. Was there such a word and if so what did it mean? I wanted a flogger's word because I was writing the song 'Fetch the Man Away' for *Ballad of Jamie Allan*:

> *fetch the man away they say fetch the man away*

and another word was needed to keep the repetition of sound from getting monotonous; I needed a slight variant of fetch. *Flech* was perfect aurally and, as I was about to find out, its meaning is straight from the flogger's arsenal. At first I looked in the OED, but it's not listed, then in an online Scottish dictionary only to be disappointed. However, when I turned to an old *Scots Dialect Dictionary* lying around my desk and compiled by Alexander Warrack in 1911, he lists *flech* with this definition:

> v. *to beat soundly; to fall upon; to scold.*

It could not be more apposite. To double-check I called Bill Griffiths and asked him to consult his Wright's *English Dialect Dictionary*. He was doubtful but he generously stopped what he was doing and gently asked me to hang on while he went and looked the word up. As the phone lay on his desk I could hear music playing quietly on the radio and Bill turning the pages of the dictionary. The word comes from Banff, he told me, and 'yi kna, the *ch* is pronounced hard, like in *loch*'. It could be no other way for my purposes.

If it comes from Banff that would place it Mid North Lowland, in the category of William Grant's dialect map reproduced by Warrack. Sadly I have never been to the north-east coast of Scotland so have no idea how such a word could make itself known. There is no memory of its currency in my childhood, which is the first place you'd want to look for a word you knew but had forgotten you knew and which had spontaneously recurred to mind. My childhood was in the North East of England and the word certainly wasn't in use there. My great-aunt Katie adopted me at the age of nine months, when I became a Pickard. But the name I was christened with was her maiden name of McKenna. Because *flech* is Scottish, albeit very specifically located, there's the possibility that my genes may have picked it up on their travels. The McKennas, originally Irish, had first settled in Scotland early in the nineteenth century and worked as miners not far from Glasgow before moving south into Northern England some generations later.

Perhaps I heard it from my great-uncle Peter McKenna who would visit when he was drunk and pick fights with my mild-mannered adopted father, a Protestant, whom I surmise from his name was a descendant of the Huguenot refugees. Uncle Peter would get a froth up on his way from the pub and by the time he reached our house was ready to flech anybody and everybody, my father in particular. However, I have no memory of his using the word. Aunt Betty, who was at least twice his size, got tired of his drunken bullying and fleched him before locking him in the coal-shed overnight, knocking his teeth out en route. They were false so it wasn't difficult and she flushed them down the toilet and told him, when she let him out next morning, that he had done it himself in his drunken stupor. If we saw him coming we would lock the door and hide behind the sofa, pretending to be out. We also hid from the priest if we caught a glimpse of his dark robes blowing up the street.

Nor was it used at my secondary modern school by the religious instructor or by the ex-military policeman responsible for the 'backward' class. They would vie with each other to flech their sullen charges for insolent ignorance with stiff cuts of pit conveyor belts until our hands were swollen and we couldn't pick up a pen for days.

> *flay him till he stays they say flech the man all day*
> *flay him in his stays they say fetch the man away*

When Natasha Vall called to say Bill Griffiths was dead I just had to get out and walk, even though a 40 mph gale was blowing.

The wind was at my back, coming from the south-west, and it didn't take long to discover that the waterproofs weren't. I made it to Black Fell where I lay amongst the rushes at the edge of a peat pool and photographed patterns created by gusts on the water's surface. Although soaked and the wind relentless I repaired gaps in the dyke with grim energy. As I built up the broken wall with piles of boulders the rough sandstone wore away at the whorls on my fingertips, erasing identity, and I realized that I was making quite a good job of it. Though always a bit slow at dyking, I was now 'clashing it up,' enough to stop the sheep from straying until a more solid build could take place. The shepherds, who travel the length of the walls on their quad bikes looking for breaks, will be confused to find the gaps mysteriously repaired, albeit temporarily. I'm like one of those elves in Grimm that mysteriously makes shoes overnight—the phantom dyker. On the way down, facing into the headwind, I kept stopping to heave a few large stones into the breeches. Rest in peace, marra.

28TH SEPTEMBER

A north-easterly and rain showers. I slipped into slut mode when I received a text from a recent ex: 'Tom would you consider this request for Sat nite? I have missed sex and I have needs. Would you help me out? I am not drunk.'

When I was walking to Black Fell a few days ago I first heard and then saw a couple of wheatears. I've not seen them for a while, just an occasional glimpse of a white rump flitting along the dyke top a few yards ahead as I walked. But I have often found an explosion of their feathers within the shadow of the dyke, where they had become a raptor's meal.

2ND OCTOBER

When I walked across the fell my animal awoke momentarily—
but tonight, when I try to sleep, all the old phantoms gather and
manifest themselves. The nagging east wind is no comfort, with
frequent and sustained inquisitorial gusts. To block thought I
tuned the radio to BBC World Service, fell into a swirling empty
slumber, then woke, sudden and afraid.

Over the previous two nights I was wooed by a smooth south-
westerly.

lying on Long Tongue
sun diffused in mist
easy sleep
without waking

3RD OCTOBER

This is the second night without pills to knock me out and sleep was intermittent, ravaged by the roar of a jet-engine wind just above my head—continuous and cold.

A range of stars and a lit city encamped on a far-away plain.

My eldest son talking on the phone from Edinburgh told me that he'd met a guy from Alston who had witnessed the Hartside Café hit by lightning the size of a football and it just bounced off the roof and rolled along the patio.

4TH OCTOBER

In bed and a pack of winds are writhing at the windows. They pass by. They gather. They whine painfully, begging in.

If there is a pin-thin gap they will take it. If there is a wormhole they will snake it. If there are eaves they will heave.

ANABATIC

at first they recce, easy
around the edge of breath

then gathered gangs unleash
and breach

but the wind has no objectives,
riding the slope of my roof

17TH OCTOBER

I'm trying to teach myself to sleep without the help of the radio to overwrite thought, with only the winds—or, rarely, silence. A silence to be feared and pursued because it is a blank canvas onto which I invariably screen my demons and because it is as easy as breath. As usual it is about 'managing' obsessions, delusions and manias—in pursuit of focused energy and calm.

A cagey early dream of an ex in the stillness of a dark night, followed by me comforting a friend as she sobbed the loss of her young son in a recent car accident.

Dawn burned in gloriously under the hill fog. When the earth tilted and the sun rose, mist thickened and I lit a fire.

Instead of working yesterday I went down into the valley mushrooming amongst the woods along the riverside and found bay and birch boletus to add to those at home. They are lying on newspapers in front of the fire sliced and drying—a double-broadside sheet of chanterelle becomes a rug of peachy yellow. I prefer to clean them while still in the woods so that I can continue to hear the rustle of the wind through silver birch leaves or the River South Tyne running steeply in the gorge below.

There is constant, often subtle, change in the landscape and in my sense of time. When I work and walk I'm most alive to myself and to the world. It's where I both lose and find myself. I'm a fells flâneur.

wind
roots in rock

water skips
undressed over outcrops

what it says
is

18TH OCTOBER

A diffused sun through mist and a tall pale sky, so I took my breakfast, a bowl of porridge, outside in the soft breeze.

When I returned Helen was working vigorously on a large aluminium pie-warmer but stopped to chat and told me that she preferred to clean outside with the weather so beautiful. I leaned against the wall, down on my haunches, as she bent over to clean the lower part of the machine, scouring it thoroughly. She talked of training as a nurse and wanting to be a midwife and that she had read a book on 'spiritual childbirth' by a sixty-year-old woman—'a bit hippy I suppose, but she has some good things to say'—about how women used to go into hospitals like battery hens. I gave her my copy of Catherine Taylor's book on childbirth in the USA. Like all the girls she'll be gone at the end of the month when the café closes—all the swallows flown. And she is swallow-like in shape and movement, or a swift perhaps—if I had to attribute a bird to her. Our conversation reminded me how long it was since I had been close to a birth and how rooting an experience it was. As she walked back inside the café kitchen she said 'I'll leave it to dry in the wind'—meaning the oven she'd just finished cleaning—and I thought how I too was drying in the wind, brushed by her swift wings as she flew past.

edge of displaced echoes
air around and sound
of bird and plane

a swallow's glittering chitter

20TH OCTOBER

What I need in this landscape is a woman. I should make a cunt-kite to fly while the moon is full above the asphalt car park on top of nowhere overlooking everywhere.

A few miles from here as the raven flies and in the late thirties Professor Gordon Manley from Durham University had a hut erected and began a study of the Helm Wind. On occasions he and his assistant were trapped by the weather and had to remain on the mountain for days until a tractor could make its way to them. His report was published in the July–October 1945 *Quarterly Journal of the Royal Meteorological Society* and titled 'The Helm Wind of Crossfell 1937–1939'. It begins:

> *The Helm Wind and its accompaniments form one example of a group of phenomena found in various parts of the world. In each case when a wind blows transverse to a range of mountains, a marked increase in the strength of the wind is noted by surface observers down the leeward slope and for a varying distance across the lowlands below, compared with that which prevails over the country as a whole . . .*

Publication had to wait until the end of the war in case it was of use to the enemy. Wind fucking in the fight against fascism.

I was two months from being born when that was published.

raggy cloud flags
lift from the hill

composition needs heat

heat of the body,
heat of fire, heat of the sun

and evaporating liquid
to rise

27TH OCTOBER

When I put my head out of the attic window all I saw was stars and the wind wrapped itself around my neck like a cold silk scarf.

Ottis has been here a few days and yesterday I took him for a walk in thick fog to the old prison house, a mile down the road, and had to carry him most of the way on my shoulders. The building, at the side of the road which runs over the top of the fells, is now used by shooters on rare occasion but it appears on old maps as 'prison house'. Apparently convicts from the east of the North Pennines were housed there overnight on their way to Whitehaven on the Solway Firth to await transportation. In sudden rough weather they would be snowed in for several days, if not weeks.

When Ottis and I climbed down the steep banks of a clough to overgrown pit heaps, to watch a fast syke, the rain became heavy and soaked us. Later, as we changed out of our wet clothes in the attic, he heard and enjoyed rain drumming the tiles and asked what's that? Then he asked about my poetry so I read him 'New Body'—*as you stroked my leopard's coat I was a tiger* ... 'It's good, that,' he said when I finished.

Later in the day we drove the six miles downhill to Alston to shop. In the chemist he was pissed off when I tried to buy a face-cloth for him and he turned to the assistant did *she* think his face was dirty because he didn't.

Read this in Coleridge's notebooks:

> *Children in the wind—hair floating, tossing, a miniature of the agitated Trees, below which they play'd—the elder whirling for joy, the one in petticoats, a fat Baby, eddying half willingly, half by the force of the Gust—driven backwards, struggling forward—both drunk with the pleasure, both shouting their hymn of Joy.*

Sad to see Ottis leave when his mother came to collect him.

29TH OCTOBER

Dream: I met a girl in London, in a small café, who was in a state of near shock. Trying to calm her I ordered a bowl of soup but she said 'you'll have to ask him, first.' *He* was a smug, nondescript middle-aged man sitting at a crowded table and looking over the top of his fork while shovelling meat into his mouth, who had been interrogating her all morning. This was only the lunch break, she implied. In fact I needed to debrief her myself as she was on the periphery of a crime that I had committed many years ago. Although I spoke boldly to the man to obtain her release from some formal but unspoken obligation she remained fearful. Her interrogation was following the progress of the same crime that I was attempting to remember for a book.

I've not been able to work on it all week, except to grab an hour and read through letters from the period, as I've been preparing papers for the bankruptcy hearing which is causing me more stress than I'd anticipated. But the outcome will free me of the telephone calls asking for payments that I can't make. Some lenders call and offer to extend the credit, but my overdraft at the bank that I use to make the minimum card repayments is exceeded, and I'm fucked.

Bankruptcy is the correct decision; hardly a decision as the other 'choice' is to be enslaved by debt and subject myself to the pursuit and ear-bashings of its bailiffs and overseers.

But the decision also means, for that period of time, leaving 'the forge', as I've come to regard my focused engagement with work, and taking the chance that it might go out—which is what I put the dream down to. I will have to be interviewed by the Official Receiver and account for all of my financial transactions over the last few years, with the risk of exposing myself to a charge of 'fraud' if they discover that I failed to declare some information to government agencies when claiming a benefit.

30TH OCTOBER

Wet and foggy. The café only opens at weekends now until the end of the month when it will close entirely for winter. The fog lifts and falls and closes in and opens up. It's an all-day tease. And very occasionally migrant redwings flock past, or a dark bird darts under the wind, hanging close to the fells, hunting or homeward.

I'm in court for the bankruptcy on Monday.

A book:

Tom Pickard: My Life in the Bureau.
The bureau within the bureau.

Thunder, and the wind sometimes so loud it's difficult to tell them apart.

a gold crest of light
caps black mountains

and a raven
on an overhead powerline

slung below cumulus

2ND NOVEMBER

Yesterday I drove to old Frank's funeral in Newcastle and his widow Pauline recalled seeing a puff of smoke coming out of a large cardboard box in her yard where her sons, Franky and Bobby, and I were smoking a Woodbine—aged three. We grew up in the same street, same school, same jail. Pauline was someone who knew the history of my—to me—mysterious origins. In the fifties and sixties old Frank worked for Robinson's Pet Store upstairs in the Grainger Market and as a young teenager I'd call in for a chat and sometimes would try to find out what he knew. All I knew was that I knew nothing outside of being illegitimate and that I had a 'brother' with the same name. Frank kept a respectful hush and probably thought that if I needed to know anything it wasn't his place to tell me. I'd always go to Franky and Bobby when there was no one and nowhere else, frequently dossing on Franky's floor in London and Bobby's in Newcastle.

After the funeral Bobby stayed with his mother and I went with the ever-restless Franky for a drink. He won't stay in one place long; when I was arrested with him in London in the mid-seventies one of the cops said they'd been exhausted when they were tailing him from bar to bar and having a drink in each. It's like he's always on the way to somewhere else. Since childhood we had developed a keen sense for undercover cops and were ever watchful in bars, especially when working, but we didn't spot those guys.

We ended up after the funeral in Rosie's Bar, which when the Morden Tower readings started was called the Northumberland Arms and was popular with bus crews who worked in the Gallowgate depot, and with prostitutes on their payday. The unlit back alley that led to the tower was close by for a quick fuck against its twelfth-century wall on top of which Franky and I used to hide when skipping off from school—discovering the ancient city in stolen time. In that bar Bunting introduced us to the dog's nose (a shot of gin in a pint of beer). The manageress was Rosie, a well-coiffured woman in her sixties who managed any and all of us, in whatever condition or mood. She would take no worky-tickets prisoner. Years later the pub was renamed after her.

Franky told me that he felt the same way about the sea that I do about the fells. Knowing how restless he is I asked how he coped with being banged up in jail for years. Yoga, he said. I can see that—if you have to do a lot of travelling while confined in one place it could enable a journey of sorts. A couple of guys he knew joined us and bought a round. One of them was tall, grey and well-built and about my age; he looked stressed and spoke to me earnestly, like the ancient mariner who stoppeth one of three, about working in some far-eastern part of Russia where he said a female welder had told him 'life fucked me.' It's very hard there, he said, many of the women have to whore and the police get a take—otherwise they lock them up for the weekend. The other guy, wound-up, agitated and puce-faced with drink and coke, asked if I was still writing communist poetry. I said, yeah; are you still mugging pensioners?

3RD NOVEMBER

Celebrate this pocket book—Begin with a Dedication to the Inventor. —Coleridge's notebooks

There's a westerly gathering its cavalry and marauding over the tussock grass and it's difficult to get warm in bed and stay warm as the cold razors its way through the covers onto my back.

4TH NOVEMBER

The blackcock that has been hanging around for a few days came to get its photo taken. The blackcock is an indigenous species that was wiped out locally, but they have been encouraged back and are despised by shooters because red grouse learn better evasion skills, watching them fly low. It comes to the patio outside my window and we watch each other as I take its pictures.

5TH NOVEMBER

A buzzard, sometimes two, hunting close to the café most of the day. Their wings upturned at the primaries and their feet frequently hanging—the undercarriage down—either by habit or in hope. Last seen at 4.30 and the light very dim.

It's difficult to keep out of bed as an icy wind is gathering its forces, sounding the tiles, whistling through gaps in the window frame.

FOR BOB

The whole sweep of the day.
If I were Creeley
I'd know what I meant
and make it a poem
but I'm not
and I don't
and I have.

A friend wondered if *the whole sweep of the day* was a line from Creeley, but it's not, as far as I know—it was just something that I wrote when I became acutely conscious of the whole sweep of the day and the possibility and impossibility of containing it in that one line at that moment. But perhaps it's a line I 'heard' from Creeley and it's just resurfaced and told me it's mine. Something like that happened in the early seventies, just after my marriage to Connie had broken down, when he read in the Morden Tower and stayed overnight in my Hubert Terrace flat on the south bank of the Tyne in Gateshead. At that time I was having a tumultuous relationship with an actress up from London for a season of Chekhov in a Newcastle rep and writing the sequence *Hero Dust*, for which I used as a legend the line *love is the highway to the door* and attributed it to Creeley; however, he denies ever having written it. The love affair had to bear the pain of separation from the kids and eventually the North, and Bob may have sensed that and come up with an impromptu line in sympathy, *love is the highway to the door*. There was no work whatsoever in the North for me and I shortly afterwards joined the drift south to doss on Franky's floor in his basement flat in London. Frank's gaff often served as a hole in the wall for pals on the trot from something or someone. On one occasion there was another Geordie staying there, either on the run or fresh from a stretch. He'd been diagnosed as schizophrenic in jail and wanted a second opinion which he got from another psychiatrist: *paranoid* schizophrenic. Franky told me that, but he may have been taking the piss.

6TH NOVEMBER

Tom Raworth sent me a pair of binoculars and I swear, as I watched a couple of cavorting ravens, there was a jump cut.

I took copies of my books in print into a fine independent bookshop in Penrith and asked the proprietor if he'd be prepared to stock them as I was a 'local' author in that I lived fifteen miles into the hills. He said leave them with me, so I did and took a ball of chalk around the town, scouring the charity shops. When I came back to collect the books and his answer he politely said, 'I'm afraid they are not suitable for my clientele.' And as I scrambled over those mounds of coffee-table eco-journals it felt as though I was escaping across the Berlin Wall and waking up in East Germany.

No support from the literary shitbags in the North East nor from those in the North West it seems. I must move north, very north, far north. Or to Ireland.

THERE'S A NORTH IN
EVERY SOUTHERN TOWN.

In angry response to Lee Hall's BBC radio documentary on poetry and the North, 'A Strong Song Tows Us', someone set up a 'more Geordie than thou' website attacking Basil Bunting, Barry MacSweeney and the Morden Tower. It's a virtual spittoon and invites contributions from the North East intelligentsia who are famous for their phlegm.

One of the invited contributors to the site asserts that Bunting was a fascist, but that comes from a willed ignorance, as any cursory glance at his biographical reputation would make clear that he was a lifelong anti-fascist, even returning voluntarily from America to join the fight at the start of WW2. As the author of that assertion, Mr Alan Brown, happened to be a teacher at the secondary school in Blakelaw where I was a pupil until the age of fourteen, it now becomes clear to me why I learnt so little; he must have stacked his lessons as he packed his satchel, full of ignorance. But I did begin to understand the language of power when we were designated *guttersnipes*, and the language of subversion when our Mr Brown became known as *Hovis*, after a loaf of sliced bread.

Leaving that school I became uncomfortably aware of my ignorance and the landscape of inverted opportunity, so sought to enrol at a College of Further Education in Bath Lane to see if I could improve my chances in the world or at least catch up on what I was meant to have learnt already. Unfortunately, because of my educational history in the lowest forms, where they dump the no-hopers, I did not meet the minimum requirements for entry and the principal could not offer me a place. But he was a reasonable man, and if I could get a recommendation from my old headmaster, he would make an exception to the rules and enrol me. All I had to do was call in to the school and ask for a reference, so I took a bus and headed there, entering for the first time by the front door—otherwise reserved for staff and visitors. The secretary told me to wait until the headmaster, Mr Millar, was ready and I hung around, as I had on so many other occasions when I was awaiting punishment.

During my penultimate year at school I began reading Shakespeare from my older sister's grammar-school books and performing it in the playground to entertain my pals. One of them told the metalwork teacher, 'please sir, Pickad knaz some Shakespeare', and he, in turn, told the headmaster that I had amused his class by hopping onto a bench to perform a verse or two. A few days later the headmaster, in his black gown and mortarboard, came into the metalwork class, something unheard of, and told us he wanted to hear the Shakespearean miracle for himself and demanded that I recite. As literature was not part of our syllabus he was genuinely puzzled—so I reluctantly agreed. After my delivery, in front of the class, he clipped a thumb under the collar of his academic gown and declaimed, like the gentleman he was—although one based on an archaic and theatrical model —a few lines from the bard, and challenged me to respond with what followed. When I couldn't he made a 'hmph' sound and walked out.

'The headmaster will see you now', said the secretary. He saw me and laughed.

'I wouldn't give any of you criminals a reference. The shipyards, or the pits—that's your future, if you're lucky—and jail if you're not.'

One night, a few years later, when the Morden Tower was drawing attention in the city, attracting large audiences of young people, and my first book of poems was published, I received a phone call from a vicar in Gosforth, where my mother had often worked as a char-wife, who asked me to perform for his youth club and I said, 'Sure, how much?'

　'A friend of yours suggested you might do it gratis.'

　'Really? Who's that?'

'A prominent member of our church, your old headmaster.'

'Well,' I replied, 'give him a message from me', and went on to surprise myself with a seething torrent of vituperation.

The website owner's justification for pissing on my dead friends is a pride in himself as an 'ideologically pure' Geordie and a *proper* poet, so I thought I'd give him voice and hear him sing:

WHINING WHILE DINING OOT

Ama propa Geordie, me
aa write propa poetry.
Nobody reads is
and it fuckin peevs is
cos ama propa Geordie, me.

Aa git funding off the Cooncil
for blaain oot me tonsils,
cos ama propa Geordie, me.
Aa gan ti matches when aa can
an wetch the team gan doon the pan,
cos ama propa Geordie, man.

Aa write propa stuff,
not like them posh puffs,
that southern tart that come up here
to write aboot her scented farts,
cos ama propa Geordie, me.
Smell the authenticity!

Aa served some time in Durham
(university).

Got a discharge with a PhD
aboot a propa Geordie, me;
not that jumped-up slug from Hull
we gets prized for being dull
aa get slavvad oot me skull,
cos ama propa Geordie, me.

If am just a smidgen posh
you know it helps is get the dosh,
aa stash it in the pigeon loft,
burrad never use a word like gosh
when I write me jangling tosh
cos ama propa Geordie, me.

Aa hoyed up with the Common folk,
but still they think that ama joke.
Will I ever get a poke?
Cos ama propa Geordie, me.

7TH NOVEMBER

A big hole in nothingness and a steady north-westerly. With the bedroom window closed it flickers insistently on the edge of awareness, an almost subliminal presence.

Worked at home until 2.30 pm—it was a struggle *between appetite and attainment.*

As I walked through the hill mist to Fiends Fell a large bird flipped over the close horizon, just high enough to reveal its underside as it peeled back below the escarpment. So light-coloured beneath and large that I thought it was a heron, but moments later a buzzard appeared in silhouette, lifting to eye level to assess the danger. When I reached the summit the raptor was gone. It had perched just below the oncoming clouds on a reclining limestone boulder patched with buzzard-coloured lichen, which offered draughty shelter from the fast cold Atlantic wind. There was another rock at its base and together they formed a rough chair so I sat and read *The Gypsy Laddie* and a few Border Ballads until the cold forced me to close the book.

'Tis not the Frost that freezes fell
Nor blawin Snaw's Inclemency;
Tis not sic Cauld that makes me numb,
But my Love's Heart grown cauld to me

The mist lifted and the sky lowered, shrouding the surrounding peaks with dark smoky blues and a band of rosy gold on the distant snow-line. As I strolled through the heather and whipped grass, stopping occasionally to gaze at the rich green sphagnum mosses, I became aware of a sudden calm. How long had the wind been silent—did I catch the very instant it stopped, or slowly become conscious of its absence? Then I heard a noise like a thin wind rising through reeds, but nothing stirred except the air some twenty feet above where I saw a fast-moving shadow, a wide massive sweep of starlings. They made no sound save thousands of wings flapping, or *flaffing* as I'd read earlier in 'Lord Thomas and Fair Annie':

There war four an twontie gray goshawks
A flaffin their wings sae wide
To flaff the stour thra off the road
That fair Annie did ride

They swept out into the mist on either side of me like the hurried rustling of a long silk dress echoing in an empty corridor. When I moved on, the winds welled up out of silence as if they'd parted to let the flock through.

Pulling a scarf across my face and my hat down to meet it I followed sheep trails towards a cairn overlooking the Eden Valley, to enjoy the gloaming from there.

As I approached the cairn a large bird silently lifted its dark form and slipped into the rising dusk. For a moment I wondered if I had seen it at all; and was it the same bird, always ahead of me, just out of sight?

8TH NOVEMBER

The officials at Carlisle County Court were polite and pleasant and the judge said, after reading my statement of affairs, 'there's no way you can pay these debts off' and declared me bankrupt. There's a 40 mph wind and the roof sounds like it's being ripped off. I drank a bottle of wine but remained sober. Time to reassess, I suppose.

The fierce wind and the hailstorm rattling at the window are a comfort. Survival from today is going to be measured and difficult because, until going bankrupt, I have used credit to support myself. Now all credit lines are dead and I have to exist on the weekly fifty-six-quid dole money and pretend to be looking for work. Basically that involves filling out what's known colloquially as *the lie sheet*, a form they supply, where I must list, Monday through Friday, am and pm, the potential employers I'm meant to have approached, letters written, phone calls made, follow-ups and follow-throughs in the search for work. Fortunately the likelihood of finding a job from this inaccessible spot seems slim. My autobiography should be called *The Book of Jobless*.

LATE START

and the day behind blinds begun

late shadows on a distant hill
a passing car

the phone rings
am I in?

9TH NOVEMBER

Sometimes I compose poems or songs in my sleep and if I am lucky wake with one still in memory. I wrote these verses in a dream and quickly scribbled them down.

She said she would not dwell
In the heather on the fell
Beneath the down upon my bed
And all the words she said.

I saw the midnight waters rise
The colour of her eyes.

I'd rather be an old stairwell
And feel the weary tread
Than be an unsprung mattress
On your old cold bed.

Hill fog and a raptor, in a 40 mph wind, hunts close to the café and hangs for long moments, tail spread, primaries upturned, feet hanging as an anchor, for drag.

Those arseholes would rather extinguish life itself than give up their power and privilege. The princes who shot the hen harriers, an animal on the verge of extinction in a country senile with centuries of servitude. We'll never be a grown-up nation until we're a republic—meanwhile we kowtow, fawn and flounce in search of favour.

I wrote that last night, a little drunk, a little stoned. It took a long time to sleep as I chased memories of my father who died this time of year, a couple of weeks before Connie—to my great joy— gave birth to Matthew when I was seventeen. When I tried to recall my father the first memory was of his last, on which he repaired the family shoes.

10TH NOVEMBER

In the flat above Jim Haynes' Paperback Bookshop in Edinburgh in 1963, when I was seventeen, I was stunned to hear Alex Trocchi and R.D. Laing in a full frontal Glaswegian face to face, graced with imaginative eloquence. I was used to listening to intellectuals talk above my head at leftist meetings, but with these two there was no manifesto to refer back to or doctrinal thesis with which to nail down thinking. They opened up more than they closed down. Later that year we invited Trocchi to read in the Morden Tower and he brought (as requested) some fine Moroccan kef, and gave a good performance, although when he began to expound 'Project Sigma' his ideas on diplomacy were at variance with Basil's who, based on his practical experience, said bollix.

Had soup next door with the lasses.

It's an icy night and my fingers are so numb I can't read in bed. When I turned off the light at ten and tried to sleep kept waking with a frozen arse. It's too cold to sleep well—at least alone. The stars are visible through the Velux window only a few feet from my head and there is thick frost on the ground and on the tiles— with puddles and pools frozen since morning. A warm female body between me and the rafters would keep the frost out of my tissues, chill out of my bones and the ice out of my blood.

11TH NOVEMBER

Wind has been raging for the last three or four nights—and foggy. Yesterday I got up sluggish, feeling down and unmotivated and couldn't work—I skirted away from the job and moped most of the day. While I was cooking soup the café owner came through with a few sell-by-date sandwiches and a vegetarian quiche which she said could be left for a couple of days. The sandwiches should be eaten the same day or binned. She also brought two large slices of apple pie.

When I was preparing the soup I walked through to the café and asked how long lentils needed to cook. Ten minutes they said— but Abbi, mischievously, told me twenty-four hours. Later she took me aside, 'I know why you live up here. It's not because of the peace and quiet; it's the food and the women. They're always saying, "Let's see if there's anything vegetarian for Tom."'

I dreamt of Ed Dorn and Bob Creeley and Ed was argumentative and Bob conciliatory. In the late sixties Jeremy Prynne was being a roadie for Ed Dorn after a gig in the tower and he drove us all— Connie, Matthew, Ed and me—to North Yorkshire to visit Tony Ward and his French wife, both novelists and both dons at University of York. They had a beautiful old stone house with a lawn running to a fast stream and they were welcoming hosts. When Jeremy offered to try and find a way to get me into Cambridge, Ed thought the suggestion wildly inappropriate and exclaimed 'oh man!' In the evening by a log fire the dope came out and Ed made a bong from a glass jar. It blew my head off.

The wind has dropped into low gear and the sun is out.

I needed to generate heat and to loosen up before work so hand-washed the large bed-cover in the bath. Wringing it out was tough. By the time I came to hang it on the line the hill was covered in a fast freezing fog accompanied by wet cloud. I hung it out anyway and was glad of the fog which gave the cover another rinse. When it eventually dries it will smell of the cold wind, as does all of my washing after being hung out. Cleaning up my life just so I can get it dirty again.

12TH NOVEMBER

Walked to Black Fell, frost on the ground and a cold north-
    westerly.
And what if you die up there? What about the poor fucks that
    have to go and get your body?
Tough on the poor fucks, I suppose. But isn't it always?

13TH NOVEMBER

How Basil was so impressed by William Carlos Williams's working arrangements. According to BB he had an attic with a desk that ran the length of it where his poems were laid out and he daily walked from one to the other making revisions. He was doing the rounds of his poems as he did the rounds of his patients and sometimes they overlapped and became part of each other.

Fierce 50 mph westerly these last few days and when it brought sleet and hailstone I woke soaked. Although the window was tight shut the wind drives the water beneath and through the tiles so that it drips and runs down onto my bed. When the wind is so fierce I usually sleep with a large sheet of plastic over the duvets. I have a chest and throat infection and the room smells damp. During the storm last night I woke from a dream where I was thrashing about violently—as violently as the wind that was shaking the roof as it tried to throttle the building.

While drying out the bedroom I thought of the nursery story of the three pigs and the wolf who tried to blow down their houses. *I'll huff and I'll puff and I'll blow your house down*. If children are meant to take practical moral guidance from the tale and build their *dwellings* of brick and stone perhaps they also take from it the wind as wolf rather than just the wolf with the power of wind in its prodigious lungs. The story may have arisen around a roaring chimney, with the windows rattling, the door shaking and the roof beams creaking as the wind howled outside like a pack of prowling wolves and the bairns cowered indoors hungry for stories.

14TH NOVEMBER

When I walked home in the frosty gloaming caught sight of a
new moon and did a quick calculation and turned to my

838th new moon

welcome
to my life

15TH NOVEMBER

Fog's thickening and a building wind is forecast to reach 60–70 mph tonight. One west-facing window is slightly open and all I can hear is a thin wind whispering through shrubs and the draw from a well-fed chimney. I've prepared a desk for work and can smell a rabbit stewing in my slow-cooker. Low grey clouds, dark fells.

I dreamt last night of Katie, my late mother, who was working with her sleeves rolled up in the café kitchen. As she'd say, she liked to get stuck in. Some of the lasses approach their work here with the same stoic resolve. Later in the dream I joined them, as I often do, sitting in the closed café by the stove, smoking after a hard day's graft.

At dusk, about four, I got cabin fever and walked quickly to Fiends Fell. It was very cold but good to see the young waxing moon low in the south. A large flock of geese flew over the pass— going towards the Solway Firth and issuing the occasional croaky honk. A honky-tonk honk.

On my return I found a weathered-out sign in one of the shooting boxes: it had originally said 'Support the good shooting code' but had weathered down to 'support ode' with a worn-out figure of someone firing a shotgun heavenwards, or it could be holding a telescope to the sky. When I got home I photoshopped and emailed it to Bobby who made me a T-shirt with 'support ode' emblazoned on it.

17TH NOVEMBER

Late last afternoon as I was sitting in the empty café eating my re-heated rabbit stew and catching the last of the light, a red car steered erratically into the empty car park and came to a halt facing the valley. The driver was the only occupant and she was quite short with what may have been a blond wig. When her door partially opened I expected her to step out but she didn't and I saw flickering lights which I thought must be the car door agitated by the gusting wind catching the last of the sun's reflections, but I was wrong. Half a minute later the woman climbed out with flaming sheets of paper about the size of a tabloid and walked backwards into the wind—holding on to and making sure that the papers burnt thoroughly. As the flames rode up in gusts she held the papers high, as though attempting to read what the fire was unwriting. She was left with one piece of unburnt paper and after studying it closely on both sides opened her grip and let the wind take it—presumably free of anything she sought to obliterate.

20TH NOVEMBER

The snow, thawed. A kestrel surfed in on a 20 mph wind, turned and hovered a few yards away from my window. Later I was visited by a lover, looking trim, with a bottle of amyl nitrate.

The space between my galley kitchen and the living room, where I've made a standing desk that I lean on to look out at the day, I call the scriptorium and have come to associate it with my father, Robert Bambro Pickard. He was a daydreamer with a gentle silence about him, a deep patience and a passion for gardening—even when in pain, as he often was, with damaged lungs and lurching after breath. The last time I saw him, he was propped upright with pillows, attached to an oxygen bottle and the life half wrung out of him on what was to be his deathbed. It was this time of year, too, in 1963.

When I was ten or twelve I carved his face with a hammer and chisel out of a large heavy piece of sandstone rock that we dug from the garden when clearing rubble. His face was already stove-in after years of ill health. My mother never quite reached five foot or the top of the washing line so she used the sculpture as a step-up. In all of the forty or so places that I've lived in the UK, I've carried it with me. It's outside now, getting greened with cloud moss. I nearly broke my back the other day carrying it over the fells to take pictures of it out there in all that free easy air he never had a breath of.

22ND NOVEMBER

Abbi came in from the café for a break yesterday and said she was leaving for Australia in a day or two. I gave her a copy of my book and a hug which she returned—holding on for a long time. I said I'd miss her and she became tearful. She may be back in February, or perhaps never.

For the second day the Eden Valley is 'flooded' with freezing fog, bringing the peaks of the Lake District mountains even closer with nothing between them and this range of hills.

A starling flew into the bushes outside my window just before sunset, but a crest made red by the setting sun revealed it to be a waxwing. Then ten minutes later a slim good-looking woman appeared in front of my window, behind the low wall, dropped her pants and peed.

The freezing fog blew up the hill and covered the café as I walked to Fiends Fell barely seeing five yards in front. The rime clung and turned me white. At the top, just beyond the trig-point I re-arranged a few stones and created another seat and shelter from (this time) the west wind and it was enjoyably strenuous. Now with shelter against winds from all directions it is possible to sit and enjoy a spliff, a hot drink from a flask and the wonders of weather at an exposed summit. I was weary, though, of sitting too long after exertion—remembering my dyking days with Jack and how difficult it was to restart after a break because of the horizontal rain, penetrating damp and sweat turned icy—which makes of the body a poor tool.

A man of action never likes to wander far from his bed.

It looks Siberian. The telephone line is down and the engineers won't be able to work at this elevation in this weather, and I'm running out of coal.

25TH NOVEMBER

I was lying naked in the attic below the low roof with a raging wind outside. There is no insulation and it's only the rattling tiles and a thin sheet of plaster that separates me from the elements. The floor shakes and my bed trembles, a woman breathing, her close warm breath and the storm's raging surge.

Woke with a cutting draught at my feet, snow on the windows—the fells covered in thick frost and a savage biting wind. I watched a buzzard hover for a while, fly off a few yards then hover again. I haven't seen a large raptor so near to the café, so I presume the cold is driving it to hunt recklessly close to human habitation. When I went outside to take pictures of frozen reeds my exposed fingers quickly numbed and drove me home. The sky darkens with a freezing fog and my toes are still numb from the brief excursion outside. A dozen redwings fly past, low and close to the ground, ahead of a rolling fog bank.

an alert kestrel slung on a gust
preens on a post

am I too old for steep cloughs, dribbling sykes,
shaking up shags in sphagnum?

a spray-whipped inverted fall
up Ayle Burn head

when mind seeks to know itself
the last place it looks is the body

26TH NOVEMBER

I dreamed that all of the streams in these hills were salt water and only the rain puddles outside the window—where I had seen my neighbour, a stoat, drinking the day before—were fresh.

Looking back up to the café at the top of the pass, covered in long thin cloud, only the outline is visible; a dark grey shadow against a light fuzzy grey. Half an hour ago the cloud was blowing in the opposite direction. At the pass long stringy clouds slip over the hillside just below the brow. They'd be scalped by the wind if any higher. Revolving blades in an icy whirlpool of vicious air.

Long scarves of cloud rise from the valleys and replicate their contours.

To amuse myself as the light was evaporating and I struggled home over a very rough fell, avoiding bog and shake-holes, I imagined Jamie Allan leading a stranger and complete novice over such a treacherous wilderness, saying: 'Follow me, but if I suddenly vanish, good luck.'

28TH NOVEMBER

Took a brief walk onto Fiends Fell and the wind from the north was like flying ice, but it was tonic; and if I can sort the heating and debt problems, I believe I can accommodate winter and pick up where I left off with my piper.

Babble stimulus: I heard this phrase on a Radio 4 doco on schizo-phrenia where they test with babble stimulus to see if anyone can hear a coherent phrase in the mix. Basically it is several layers of speech laid slightly off-kilter so that no single word is audible ex-cept to someone who is likely to 'hear voices'.

The café is now closed for the winter.

there's a puckering purr from the fire,
a gust of wind and gurgling grouse

the earth turns over a day
as a pitched raven, swept aloft,
cuts low on an uprush

a breath of grass
slicked by quick light

midges yoyo on a thread of sun

The way cloud streams slowly over the hill and down into the valley turns the landscape into an animal changing shape, curling into silent dusk under a cool silk blanket. There's a degree of madness required to live here and survive; mine is to understand the weather and location a little better and 'bond' with it and with the day. It's like learning to live with a community of wild animals, sometimes reassuringly calm, sometimes threatening to eviscerate, rip flesh from bone.

30TH NOVEMBER

When Mesolithic children's graves were opened in Norway archaeologists found tongue-shaped stones in their mouths.

Let the mouth discover, talk falls apart on the tongue.

I got up early and lit the fire but, because I had miscalculated the number of sticks needed to kindle, it went out after a few moments of glory when the wind drew the burning paper too quickly. However, when I lit the café log-stove I was a bit more scientific, or focused perhaps, and succeeded. Now, in the attic again, at the 'captain's log book' and it's gusting between 40–50 mph; it reminds me how often I have gone to sleep with a sense of imminent danger when the tiles rattle, the window and door-frames shake and the floor and walls tremble. Last night when I went to bed I decided to 'face my demons' again, and instead of the unconscious dialogue that would sometimes occur with the radio at an almost subliminal level to enable sleep, I listened to the wind instead.

LA VITA NUOVA XXXV

I started to look rough and feel worse, like a dosser
And thought I'll never score like this.
Just then . . .

I wonder if there is a good modern version of LVN, because the two that I'm reading by D. G. Rossetti and Barbara Reynolds are sometimes awful. Reynolds in the poetry while her prose is clear, and DGR floral and inverted in his prose but occasionally his verse breathes easy. I suppose he's sticking to a measure—but it's trying. 'It's my party and I'll cry if I want to.' I keep thinking of pop songs when reading LVN.

When I went into the baker's in Alston L was serving and I asked how she was.

'Still looking for a decent bloke to shag' she told me.

'What kind of pasties do you have?'

'Cheese and onion or spicy lentil.'

'I'll have the spicy lentil'

'Good choice'

'Do you recommend it?'

'The spicy lentil?'

'The shag.'

'Cheeky bugger! But, yes. I do.'

1ST DECEMBER

After making the room warm and myself covered like a caveman
against the draughts, I worked in the attic at the old school desk
for a couple of hours. A very fast easterly rattled the roof a few
feet above and at 2.30 I decided to walk. It took about three quar-
ters of an hour to prepare—making sure that the fires were safe,
packing a notebook, pens, cameras, securing the house and dress-
ing to meet very rough weather. Once out I headed up to Black
Fell with a 40 mph wind at my back making the ascent easy.
When I reached the summit the wind was up to 60 mph and I
flew in it, leaning into the valley with my arms outstretched and
my coat held open like a leathery old bat. It was four o'clock and
too late to take pics of the billowing grey clouds swept by time.
Coming back into the wind was hard unless I had the option of
walking below and behind the dykes that gave shelter from the
relentless gale. Even though it was getting dark and dangerous
underfoot I couldn't resist the temptation to bend over and lift
my lugs out of their tight covering, to hear the easterly howling
through the gaps and over the top of the wall. The notion of shel-
ter becomes intense when weather rages a few feet overhead and
all around.

I kept the log fire burning in the café all day yesterday in preparation for tonight's party, and when I called Bob in Newcastle and told him, he said he'd never been to a staff party before, 'but if I had we'd all be in a pub wearing balaclavas.'

2ND DECEMBER

When I'd lit the wood stove in the café before dawn to try and
generate heat for the party three of the lasses arrived and began
to prepare food for the evening meal and set the tables and when
they finished left to get into their glad rags for the shindig. The
guest list for the meal was limited to those who worked in the
café part or full time throughout the year, thirty in all. After
the meal, when the dishes were cleared away, friends and family
would be welcome for the drink, the craic and a dance, and many
of them drove up the steep winding often foggy roads on either
side of the escarpment.

As I had been in residence for five months I was invited to join
the party, but I'm a shy bloke and faced with walking into a room
of relative strangers for a formal meal, hesitated. The last time I
had been invited to a neighbour's party was in 1972 when I lived
in a near-derelict ground-floor flat in a two-story Gateshead end
terrace house on the banks of the Tyne.

> *this street is built with bricks*
> *of furrowed brows*
> *whole gutters explode*
> *and tremble with sparrows*

My upstairs neighbour, Jenny, a pale thin single mother in her twenties whom I'd only seen occasionally and never spoken to, knocked on my back door and asked if I'd like to come to a party that night and could she borrow my Jimi Hendrix LPs which she'd obviously heard playing as I lay in the flat below her chilled with a chillum. Later, after collecting a few bottles, I prepared a couple of skinny single-skin spliffs and dressed to party with jeans, black jacket, a white shirt and slim black tie—ready to dance as I did on Wednesday nights in the Workingmen's Club that rented its upstairs room to the Rock and Roll Club and to which Teddy boys, black angels, bikers and bar-room bats shook their frocks and locks to the rock.

Before I climbed the external stairs to knock on Jenny's back door I paused to listen, to gauge how lively the party was, but there was silence. When she opened the door there was only herself and the friend she worked with in the teddy-bear factory just opposite, whose owner was our landlord and from where the rats which invaded our flats came. The 'factory' was really a late-Victorian warehouse, blackened with a century of grime from the armaments factories and engineering works which lined the river on both sides, and where you could imagine a Dickens tragedy set. After sitting down uncomfortably and popping a bottle during an intermittent but brittle silence there was a conspiratorial knock on the door and the girls looked nervously at each other and I began to wonder what kind of party it was going to be. A heavily built guy came in wearing working clabber and his face dirty from grafting in the coke works, but beneath the grime a bloodshot and cut eye from a very recent beating was visible. As Vicky's lover took a can out of each of his pockets she said 'he gave him such a kicking' and he said 'I need a wash.'

'Jenny, would it be ok?' asked Vicky already on her way into the bathroom with her lover. Vicky was unhappily married to a long-distance truck-driver and had blagged Jenny into letting her use the flat as a love nest. When that became clear and the bottles emptied and I was appointed her babysitter I invited Jenny down to my place and she was pleased to leave, although she felt that her friend had pulled a stroke; 'Vicky's husband might find oot. I don't want any more nutters banging on me door.'

We got into bed but she wasn't comfortable making love, so we talked by the fireside and she told her story.

> It only lasted two weeks
> then I couldn't stand the sight of him.
> He knew I didn't love him
> but he married is out of pity.
>
> The Social Security summoned him
> for desertion. I told them
> I didn't want owt off him.
> They went mad in court.

But it's not his bairn,
and I don't want his money.
I just want to be left alone.

The doctor gave is some pills,
but I get agitated and can't get done.
Then I get ratty with the bairn and think,
I'll kill him and there's nobody here to stop is.

I was lucky getting the flat.
But there's rats from the dery' factories.
I found one on his cot.
They come for the crumbs
and eat their way through a loaf.

The council put doon poison.
I hope he doesn't find it.
He eats like a horse, the little get;
he eats more than I do.

Me sister said she'd take him
if her man gets a start down in London.
She thinks the world of him, mind,
and he'd be happy with her.
But ad miss him.

At about two in the morning she told me that she'd been a harrier several years ago so I challenged her to a race. She flew ahead of me over the High Level Bridge to Newcastle and round by the Forth Goods Yard, where my father had worked as a porter, then back across the Redheugh Bridge along empty streets glowing with amber river mist.

'If that sod left me in peace' was her occasionally muttered mantra referring to her ex who had found out where she lived and hammered on her door at all hours, calling hoarsely through her letterbox *I know you're in there, open the fucking door*. She later told me that he and his pal were being charged with attempted murder.

One day, shortly after I moved into the ground-floor flat beneath hers, he came into our shared backyard and up to her back door and began pounding on it. I could hear her moving quietly above, obviously hiding. He'd chosen to come through the yard because the back of the house faced the near-derelict teddy-bear factory and was not otherwise overlooked. It worried me as Jenny's door, like mine, wasn't too secure and as he continued to bang and then kick, I didn't want to confront the raging beast directly, so went out into the yard with a chopping axe and said in a good-buddy way, 'howz it gannin, kidda?' Then before he could answer I ripped a plank off my coal-shed door and began chopping it, violently. Splinters flew and the hinges whined as I ripped off a second plank. He gave another loud knock to Jenny's and hung around until I had systematically axed the coal-shed door into kindling before he finally left.

As the lasses were gathering in the café for the staff party I cleaned up, shaved, and put on a shirt and jacket and the same slim black tie. When I tentatively poked my head around the dividing door a couple of the lasses gave a cheer and escorted me to the kitchen for a serving of the meal that had been cooking all day and a frequently refilled glass of wine.

The trajectory of my role as an unofficial caretaker had begun when I discovered one night, after the café had closed and everyone gone home, that a ground-floor window had been left open in the café bathroom and it was visible from the road. Even I felt tempted to climb in, so I was certain that any passing scally would not be able to resist, especially given the location—from which on a clear day or night any approaching vehicle can be spotted several miles away in either direction. After a tough day when the café closes the lasses wash the dishes and pans, put food away safely in the fridges, scrub every surface and floor, and for the last job clean the customer toilets. By then they're often knackered and someone sometimes forgets to close a window before locking up. The owner lives down in the valley and wasn't keen to come back and open up the café—so I cat-burgled in, closed the window behind me and unlocked the dividing door between my accommodation and the café which was normally kept locked from their side, but after a few more occasions when I had to draw on my Geordie genes and hoik myself through the window and through the café, she thought it expedient to give me a key so that I could ingress and egress with ease. From then on I began to check the windows and doors every night after the café closed and the lasses had left.

With the positioning of the chairs and tables around the fire it could have been a tribal gathering and Colin and Kath, the café owners, like Border chieftains surrounded by friends and neighbours. There was a lot of food and drink, but the evening was touched with death; some months earlier a young son had been killed in a motor accident.

It was a tender time to get drunk on the hilltop, with a 50 mph gale lashing the building and, as the lasses danced, dressed in their splendid best, to Rue and the Rockets playing limp melodies or jumping rock classics which lacked a spark plug or two, I realized how the year was coming round again and how we dancers on top of the hill, with the raging wind and our dervish-like whirling, willed the world to turn and keep turning.

4TH DECEMBER

A 60 mph westerly roaring and gusting to 70 assailed the bed and I couldn't get warm and hardly slept. I have to devise a strategy.

Downstairs the rats which chewed their way through the rotten door-frames have nested in the house somewhere close to my galley kitchen, judging by the faint smell I can't find the source of. They're coming off the fells seeking shelter for winter.

I took part in a successful robbery with Franky and the late Eric Mottram who was driving, rather ineptly, the getaway car. A girlfriend on bail suggested we move to London. 'But what about the winds?' I said. When she came to bed I slipped easily into her and woke with a stiff cock to the splattering of rain on the tiles and the quick breath of wind slapping the roof.

In 1650 Basho, on his journey into the deep north, is forced by a storm to lodge overnight in a cottage with two prostitutes. They discuss wind as an aphrodisiac; how it can eroticize dreams, or when making love becomes a third presence—sometimes a silky masseuse whose hair brushes air over skin, or a deranged husband howling at the window.

HOMAGE

a stripper strokes the
slope of her hip; Hokusai
painting Mount Fuji.

5TH DECEMBER

After a home visit and an interview to establish the legitimacy of my claim, the Housing Benefit people have exposed a half-truth, and if they think they have sniffed a rabbit and decide to give chase my mixed metaphor is cooked.

Otherwise I am getting out each day despite the weather and feeling something approaching cheerful.

When I opened the bathroom window I caught a whiff of wet air, the sound of a quiet but determined teenage wind and an anxious anticipation of snow. The fells fall silent when it snows, and in the backyard filling a bucket with coal the only other sound melts on contact with gutters running into drains.

A body warm, fed and watered and a constant awareness of the weather protects against intimidation. As I write that sentence a cloud drifts up from the valley with two sleek peregrines surfing its crest. A dreaming landscape and defining falcon. The silence of a predator and of its petrified prey.

When a fierce wind sucks flames furiously up the chimney I feel like a stoker, throwing fuel to keep the engines pumping for a fast ship at sea. Or like a fireman on a roaring steam train shovelling through the night. There's an incredible almost manic energy required of the stoker to match the energy of the storm—as though feeding it. But the reality is I generate more heat when throwing coal onto the fire than the fire gives out when burning it.

6TH DECEMBER

The day begins when I clear out the ashes and light a fire. A flock of geese head over the Eden Valley for the Solway estuary. A cock blackbird eats berries from the bush outside my window where a stoat has utilized the rat's run. It's a very cautious, nervous creature, making quick exploratory dashes. The wind last night like a steady sea breaking on a shoreline.

These drifting misty days are so dreamy.

7TH DECEMBER

Swollen glands in the throat again—possibly because I walked up to Black Fell yesterday in a cold fast wind. Pissed off, as my energy levels drop steeply with pharyngitis, if that's what it is.

> *wind at a chimney lip*
> *plays the flue*
> *like a sooty flute*

Sometimes the wind seems like an enveloping orgasm that I'm being tossed around in. Sometimes riding, sometimes ridden. Then it's breathing.

the emptiness
of winter fells

claws of cloud grip a far hill
topped in snow

a raven croaks

11TH DECEMBER

Blue these last few days, and woke that way this morning and would have stayed in bed, but the slut hill opposite was flouncing her wares—mist veil tinged with dawn—so, still groggy, I grabbed my camera, made a flask of hot cocoa and honey, set the fire for easy lighting on my return and headed across the crispy snow up into the clouds of freezing fog.

The early sun began to burn through small patches here and there, but when I reached the summit, shadows slid across the slopes of far fells and gathering hill mist rode up outstretched Long Tongue like a silk stocking.

On the ascent I found myself thinking of you and continued the conversation while sitting behind a dyke in the lee of the wind as freezing fog persuaded me get up and leap from tussock to tussock to keep warm until it rolled back and a liquid sun momentarily burnt through enough heat for me to lean on a dyke and write to you again—whoever 'you' are.

> *how would I know you if I could?*
> *how should you know me if you would?*

Running home, in a hurry as the temperature quickly drops, the sun goes down and the moon fills out and I think with my feet as I hop from tuft to turf.

12TH DECEMBER

When lead-miners resisted the owners' introduction of a time-keeper in mid-nineteenth-century Allendale they were locked out. It was a completely alien way of thinking, to how they related to time, to work, the earth and our place on it. It was a continuation of enclosure, but this time of the mind. A slave-owner's mindset—ownership and enclosure with threat of exclusion ensures compliance. Some of the miners and their families became emigrants and settled in Chicago and parts of Australia.

Swollen glands in the throat, ulcer playing up, total lack of energy. Heavy wind and rain, low cloud, little light. The fire is burning and its flames are sucked up the chimney before giving out much heat. But, it's a privilege to be here, on top of the fells, at all times and in all weather.

Dreamt an old raven warned me not to talk to a woman, but I disobeyed and was attacked by black swifts the size of crows, sleek and fast. Quite a fairy-story dream.

Heard today of a funeral in Alston, of Miss Bonnie, who was a self-proclaimed witch. She was a friend of Aleister Crowley and settled in Alston Moor decades ago. When I asked about her papers I was told they'd been burnt, in fear or respect, along with pictures of her with Crowley.

15TH DECEMBER

As I sat in my homemade shelter on top of Fiends Fell the sun appeared from behind a dark low cloud just as a hawk caught sight of me at the last moment, only feet away. It came so close that I could feel the whisper of its wings as it suddenly banked above my face.

16TH DECEMBER

My sister Sadie called last night to tell me Tom Pickard had died. One of his daughters broke the news to her saying their wish was that only the two daughters attend the funeral and no flowers. Sadie was upset about it, 'after all he was our brother.' She'd telephoned his old people's home a few years ago to make contact but Tom didn't want to talk, he rarely did. Because I was in the habit of occasionally calling on him when passing his book-stacked hut up the yard from Miller's sale-room in Gallowgate, he formed the erroneous impression that I thought he was my natural father, mistaking a younger brother's grudging admiration and desire for approval—something of a lost cause—he eventually told me that my natural mother was Ella McKenna, whom I believed to be my aunt until that moment. All he knew of my father was that he was a Canadian soldier stationed during WW2 near my mother's unit. Tom often bought anything odd or old that he thought he could sell and frequently recalled just missing an original John Martin painting. While he told me who my natural mother was, I picked up half a human skull that had been turned into a drum with skin stretched across it. I never thought to ask if it was also human.

From when I was barely a teenager Tom would take me to jumble-sales and encourage me to push through to the front of the scrum and grab as much as I could of what looked re-sellable. And I would often end up squashed against a trestle table or a wall by a crush of large women wearing headscarves and smelling of sweet sticky sweat, fighting to reach the bargains which lay on the tables behind which stood anxious middle-class women in charge of selling, nervous of the hefty scrum. The books I was meant to look out for and grab were old or with an index and bibliography.

Later, when I left school and home, he offered to set me up with a barrow in the Bigg Market in the centre of Newcastle to sell second-hand books, which I did for a short while. He once talked me into buying thirty copies of *Teach Yourself English for Swahili-speaking People*, thinking that I would be stuck with them and it would discourage any further forays into his business; but I got rid of the lot in one go and at a decent profit to another bookseller, Robinson's in the Grainger Arcade, who asked if I could get more.

Tom's resentment wasn't about an incursion into his book-dealing territory so much as the wearing of his name. The awareness of the absurdity of two brothers with the same Christian name came slowly because I had grown up with it and thought it normal, but he must have felt resentment from the moment of my adoption by his parents, my great-aunt and uncle. How often did he have to explain why his younger 'brother' bore the same name? 'Our Ella's bastard' might have been an answer.

> *Kicking around my pram contentedly at the age of two months in 1946, taking in an early crisp and cloudy spring, when a new face—topped with a sailor's hat bearing the inscription HMS Vanguard—looked curiously into my lair and rattled the bright red plastic balls suspended from an elastic string stretched out in front of me.*
>
> *'Big ears hasn't he?'*
>
> *It was Tom Pickard home from the war. I didn't know it then but I was soon to be Tom Pickard too.*

The intrusion into his life peaked when I was in deep debt and an enterprising bailiff looked up my name and found Tom's address attached to it, went to his house and demanded payment which was refused. Tom and his wife justifiably resented it, and unfortunately that was one of many bailiffs banging on their door in the mistaken belief that they had found me.

17TH DECEMBER

A razor-slashing easterly breathes ice between gusts.

A lover visited Saturday night and we drank wine, smoked grass, fucked and sniffed poppers. When I slid beneath the duvet the bottle spilt and I was breathing pure amyl until I fell out of bed and lay trapped against the wall in a paroxysm of hilarious overwhelm.

Looking though an old notebook I found these:

you fell asleep
as the sun slid up slates

your clothes on the floor
and thighs still damp

your scent distils memory
as the road ahead opens

*

I have no story
Simply this
My existence measured
In a kiss

I have no story
We were born to die
Lay me down
Between your thighs

18TH DECEMBER

Coming home in the gloaming, fast-hopping over bog, lowping side to side across long stretches between tufts and making a quick decision—mid-leap sometimes—where to plant my feet when they land.

The older I get the more time I want to spend in the hills—so winter-silent now.

I began to think about Jamie Allan's one-time partner, Nell Clark, who was hung and anatomized with her sister for the robbery and murder of eighty-year-old Maggie Crozier, the inhabitant of The Raw, a remote bastle on the English–Scottish border. William Winter, who was with them, was hung and gibbeted close to the scene of the crime. I found the depositions relating to the trial in the National Archive.

THE RAW

A razor wind slashed as she douked below dykes,
following dips and shake-holes, taking detours along dales.
Her skirts tacked the storm that stropped her face
with the icy edge of a blade.

High Carrick, Elsdon, Late May 1791

When her daughter Jane fell sick Jean Clark asked Isabel
if they could board in a barn,
and begged milk for her up and down the road for days.

Three months later she called in to light her cutty pipe
as Isabel's mother, Maggie, was leaving
with a bundle of merchandise to sell from The Raw.
Jean asked 'does your mither sell more than baccy?
And does she live in yon muckle hoos hersel?'

William Winter, just back from a seven-year stretch
in the Hulks, met the Clarks at Edington Mires
and travelled to Stannerton Heugh, where they camped.

Jean told him they were penniless
but when she'd bought baccy at The Raw
she saw fifty guinea worth of goods on the table.
And she knew the way 'brawly.
The lasses can tek ye there.

'Gan by Black Heddon, Little Harle, and Kirkwhelpington,
north owa the moors, across the Elsdon turnpike to Whiskershiel.
Then meet me and the grandbairn at Huntlaw the morra.'

Nell and Jane left with Winter
who stole a sheep and killed it,
then got a coulter in a haugh field near Little Harle.

Whiskershiel Fell

A merlin harried a singing lark over a chased sky.
It flipped and dived without missing a note.

Young Abraham, tending his master's flock,
climbed a steep slope to a sheepfold
where Nell and Winter were girthing an ass
and saw Jane wrap a large gully in straw rope.

Fresh-picked sheep bones lay scattered in the heather.

When he saw Abraham, Winter
sang a few lines about a shepherd boy
and asked 'whet o-cleck is it?'

Jane led away, north over the moor towards East Nook,
to a narrow clough where they fastened the ass to a dike
and waited for the lights in the hoos to gan oot.

The Raw

Shadows flit across the vaulted ceiling
to a high winding jig that pipes through every crack and gap.
The isolated bastle was exposed to the sweep of a reiving wind,
drilling the shell of her home with the bit of its beak.

Winter used the coulter to jemmy a gap between door and jamb
and pulled back a wooden bar to get in.
The sisters, lying on each side of her, held Maggie still
while he broke the locks off two chests and a cupboard
and took lawn, silk handkerchiefs, cambric
and fifteen yards of blue shalloon.
And from a small chest seven gowns,
nine bed gowns, fifty yards of red, blue, black
and spotted ribbon.

He took an old striped petticoat from the bed head
and from the cupboard four or five pounds of white thread,
nine pair of women's white cotton stockings,

two pounds of currants and raisins and half pound of starch.
From a drawer in a dresser he took one dozen handkerchiefs
and shawls and a piece of cut cheese and bread.

The sisters held Maggie down while he fetched the gear out.
When he came back for them Jane said 'she's got coin',
and showed him a hidden pocket near Maggie's head.
But Winter said 'it's time to gan and if yi divint I'll skelp yiz.'

He went to the bedside but old Maggie was still.
He took hold of her shoulders and shook her.
He raked the fire to make a flame. Lit a candle
and found a cut on her face, and a handkerchief
drawn around her neck
and tied with two knots.
He raised her and laid her down again.
He threw cold water.

'You've done bad lasses, she'll not speak again.'
They put the gear in sacks on the ass's back
and set out for Kirkwhelpington
but got lost in the dark and sheltered behind a hay pike
where they ate bread and cheese,
and gave the ass some green peas
found amongst the swag.

At daybreak Jane pulled on a pair of blue stockings.
Winter said they'll get you hung;
but she wouldn't take them off,
she didn't care.

They arrived at Kirkwhelpington,
close to eight in the morning.
The sisters drank a dram of rum with ale
and Winter, three drams and a tankard.
He told Nell keep an eye on the ass.

The Raw

When Barbara Drummond called at The Raw
and got no answer she went and fetched Elizabeth
who found a coulter on the stair head
and a broken bolt forced from the door.

The gaff was rummaged—chests open and empty,
draws out, petticoats pulled across the floor.

They lit a candle and found old Maggie
with a wound under the right eye,
a scratch on her neck and a fracture with depression
on the left temple. The jugular veins were turgid;
and there was a swelling under the left ear
where a red-and-white-spotted handkerchief
was tied tight, with two knots.

When the blankets were pulled back
a large cooper's gulley fell from the bed.
It had a wooden haft and blooded blade.

Black Bull

Jordan, of the Black Bull in Stamfordham, bought off old Jean
fifteen yards of blue shalloon,
some lawn, some cambric and two handkerchiefs,
one of which she tied around her daughter's neck.

Next morning, before six,
they crossed the Tyne at Wylam Boats
and slept on Bar Law. On Thursday Jean told Winter
'Jordan wants a dozen cheeses and a butter firkin or two,
if you can get them.'

He crossed the Tyne again, with Jane,
and just before midnight went to a house
between Acomb and the Hermitage
and robbed a fleece of wool
and two wooden bowls from a byre.

Nell in Jail

When I visited Nell I thought she would be terrified of the hanging but she was more afraid of the public dissection that was to follow.

'They're ganna gut me like a rabbit.'

'You'll be past caring', I told her.

'What will they be looking for, Jamie?'

What could I tell her? She paused for a minute.

'A bag of shite is all they'll find in me sister.'

We laughed at that.

'Will you play, at the hangings?'

I told her no.

'Why not?' she insisted.

'What should I play, then?'

'You decide.'

'A jig?'

She laughed bitterly. 'Same old Jamie.'

'They won't want to hear a lament. Not for you, Nell.'

'Well, give them their fucking jig. You may as well get a meal out of it.'

'I have no stomach for it.'

'Since when?' she flung at me.

I rose to leave.

'Aye, run away when it gets awkward, like you always do.'

'Do you remember the tune you played on the road to Newcastle, when I first went with you?'

The first and the last, I thought.

'Dorrington Lads', she recalled. When I finished playing it she wept. It was the only time that I have seen her do so. When she finished sobbing she drew a shawl over her throat and her body shuddered. Eventually she spoke and her voice was steady.

'We should have stayed together, we made a good team.'

I couldn't help but turn to the scaffold and when she caught my involuntary glance we both laughed. After a while she said: 'There's one like that waiting for you, Jamie Allan. But one of your gentlemen will speak up, say what a rare specimen you are and plead and get you aff. They always do.'

'Why do we fight, Nell?'

'Not for much longer.'

'Your mother used to say, "What's five minutes hanging to a year of pleasure."'

'Does it take as long that?'

Then she held a silence between us for a long time, looking back at me from a far distance.

'You'll not always be so lucky.'

19TH DECEMBER

A raven was forced by a peregrine to land close to the window. When the raptor left the raven took off and resumed its journey up towards Black Fell. Shortly afterwards another raven flew by en route uphill. I presume it's the same pair that I have been seeing on most of my walks. I wonder if they anticipate me as I do them? Colin Simms thinks a family of ravens know him when he 'meets' them on the fells. He certainly calls up to the oldest and largest bird the way he would greet an old hill farmer.

Walking along a familiar track I caught myself thinking pretty much the same thought that I did last time in that place and wondered if specific thoughts occur or become associated with a particular place through habit—or maybe it takes so many physical paces away from base to begin the unravelling or shaking up of thought in a particular order. Does thought occur in order? It takes physical movement to unpack, I find.

Once past the cairn the weather came in quickly from the valley and was already at the foot of Watch Hill so I turned back, getting only moderately wet by the time I reached the café. Then rain hit the south side of the house and turned to snow, thick sloppy flakes that slid down the glass to build a curtain.

wind-driven rain
hits the window

a rush of nipples
ripping silk

20TH DECEMBER

This morning I woke from a dream of an incident with cobblers who, when asked, said they could easily replace the soles of my walking boots—which, as it happens, are treadless. I've always loved that painting by van Gogh of his old boots (and the one by Magritte too) and take great care of mine.*

The wind suddenly dropped at midday and it feels like spring. Five ravens flying directly into the sun and so low overhead that I was able to hear their stiff wings flaffing.

---

*The doctor tells me that I have Morton's metatarsalgia. It's like having a stone in my shoe and I can't walk without agony so I'll have to have surgery. Perhaps I should try to read my dreams more carefully.

21ST DECEMBER

Another dry bright day with a young easterly blowing and I climbed to Black Fell and sat against a dyke at the summit with my back to the low winter sun to drink hot soup. Before the flask was opened a merlin flew low and fast towards me without altering course, up from a northern slope, a yard from the ground, close and silent as it sliced the air, flashing past. I looked into its face for the fraction of a moment I saw it.

When I got home I discovered that one of my Wellington boots lying on its side near the door had some tissue paper pushed into the toe and a plastic bottle top the size and shape of a thimble. The mice were back and it wasn't good news, but I was touched by the thought of the creature making its home in my boot. It's not difficult to imagine, in times long gone, someone attributing such mousy labours to a thumb-sized cobbler.

22ND DECEMBER

The wind is getting energetic, into the high twenties, with a thunderous roar like a low-flying warplane over my bedroom roof.

Mist covered the Eden Valley as I came back from Black Fell last Friday, so I leant against a dyke and took pictures, framing the mountains in mist like Chinese paintings where only the outline is visible and the rest a blank canvas. As I stood behind the dyke with my fingertips frozen, framing the landscape and trying not to peer for too long into the low gold sun, I became aware of another creature, a large bird, sitting on top of the same dyke two hundred yards away. My useless binoculars wouldn't work so I tried to take a picture at the end of the camera lens, leaning on the wall to steady the shot. Fortunately I was in deep shadow and the bird appeared to be unaware of my floundering with broken or inadequate equipment. After a few moments it took off upwind, over the valley, hunting. The moon was in the north-east and the sun as far south-west as it gets. If I faced over the wall the bird might fly into frame with the valley of mist—or the hurricane of gold that was the sun—but if I stayed where I was, sunk into the shadows, it might fly into and share a frame with the moon.

Sitting on the frosty moss and heather behind a bush of rushes and leaning against a loose dyke as the wind sliced through I watched the buzzard hunting in the last light—hanging in air, sweeping methodically above the hillside to hover before finding another perch to watch and listen and measure its energy. After ten minutes it took off and in a short time it had crossed high over Raven Beck and into the Croglin Valley.

a snapping collie
herding clouds across
a full moon

23RD DECEMBER

As I was trying to create some order in my cabin, I picked up *The Unquiet Grave* by Palinurus, which was given to me by Lindsay Anderson in 1976. Reading Connolly's introduction reminds me how his recognition and promotion of *Briggflatts* in *The Sunday Times* was so pivotal in winning a wider readership for that poem, and for Basil. I was struck by his reason for writing the book at all. 'As a man [Palinurus—i.e. himself] he was suffering from a private grief—a separation for which he felt to blame . . .'; just as one of *Briggflatts*' themes is remorse for deserting a lover, and perhaps love.

The wind was animated last night and I dreamed I was part of a family and outside by a strangely warm, snow-covered river-bank. Showered in blossom we walked over the frozen river.

as it comes in
and goes out
the day opens
and falls back
on itself

you can't help
but be
in it

24TH DECEMBER

A west wind has been blowing all night and the snow is melted. I didn't sleep too well and dreamt of a murder. All I remember was talking to someone with the bloody axe in my hand. Shades of Raskolnikov.

My attic bedroom is a gable end with three exposed walls facing south, east and west. I say walls but only the gable could be called a wall—the others are the two sloping sides of the roof. In this attic cabin, at this desk and in this journal I log the changes as though I were sailing a course and charting as I go, everywhere and at once, then nowhere.

The wind roars above and around, strumming an overhead power line. My Aeolian harp.

25TH DECEMBER

Misty, damp underfoot. When I went outside for a bucket of coal I could smell the damp earth and immediately caught a gasp of wind which drew my focus inward and outward at the same time, so I came up to my *cabin* to hear every breath—now a long sigh, now a few short sweeps.

that space
to go to
to get out of it

a sea of grass
picked off
by quick light

and rapid
agitation

26TH DECEMBER

There's no cloud and no moon and I stayed on top of Black Fell until Venus got out of bed, then stumbled home over frosted tussock in her light. Although the Milky Way was a spread web she was the brightest object.

cold clear light
frost on the roof tiles
and crisp air

27TH DECEMBER

Friday, 11 am. I'm in bed late to save on coal as it's a fast wind topping 30 I'd guess, but certainly fast enough to suck the fire's heat directly up the chimney. Two nights ago I was kept awake waiting for the roof to come off and in a half sleep made a list of what I could save if it did. Then I heard a loud bang and discovered in the morning that my chimney-pot had blown off and smashed onto the tiles only a few feet over my head. The house is being torn apart; 45 mph gusts are shaking the roof now.

The morning sky grey and fast. Pale golden fells.

A buzzard flew close to the café, hanging in air, hunting. Later, to the accompaniment of a Strauss waltz playing on the radio, two ravens blew into the fast wind and flipped over, dropped a few metres before flipping back to regain height and then repeated the performance.

Heaving rain, driven from the west, rides up the window and stays there.

28TH DECEMBER

I have a habit of preparing my bed and bedroom as though expecting a lover. It's a 'good' habit even if no lover is expected or exists. But there will be a lover and she could walk into my life at any time. I just have to make sure that I'm there when it happens.

A south-easterly is getting up slowly and Long Tongue to the north is so seductive—bright and gradually opening to pale wintry blues. However, a freezing fog is travelling up the valley from the south like a malevolent army whose outriders steal ahead, up the gullies to outflank the hill.

A relentless rippling tide edging itself forward until everything is absorbed and overwhelmed.

29TH DECEMBER

I tend to wake these days with a sense of dread. And it doesn't help to have 4x4 fuckwit boy racers skidding round the car park in their matching motors until midnight. The owner of the café sometimes fails to lock the café door and that's a worry. Perhaps it is time to leave this place—but where to go and how to get there?

30TH DECEMBER

I woke sobbing. The wind was fast, one gust clinging to the tail of its predecessor all night and as I write. There is snow falling and it covers everything. The electricity keeps cutting out.

Rereading Kafka's *The Trial* and K's obsession with his case—when he meets and debriefs the travelling salesman in the advocate's office—reminds me of remand prisoners in Brixton, myself included, continually and obsessively exploring every interpretation of the evidence against them and the possible outcomes of their trials.

> *silence*
> *inside the cloud*

NEW YEAR'S DAY

the blizzards blown out
snow blowers go below
sun-white Watch Hill

a growking raven groaks
my first foot flying past

2ND JANUARY

Delayed lighting the fire because the wind is so fierce that it will burn buckets of coal too quickly and I still owe for the last delivery. Inevitable draughts in the attic but it's ok to work there with a whole sheepskin wrapped around my middle. Gale all night and roaring overhead now. I have to fight off a wish to sleep through most of this cold damp dramatic weather; however, I have been reading, while working on Jamie Allan, Giles Oakley's *The Devil's Music: A History of the Blues*, to get a sense of the life of itinerant musicians from a rural background, and came across this description of loud-mouthing: 'at their most rudimentary they were little more than a strident lament, in which every phrase was exploited purely for its sound qualities in empty air ...'

4TH JANUARY

Before lighting the fire yesterday I walked out into the gale to Black Fell. It kept blowing me sideways but once at Hartside Heights I could walk behind the dyke which broke the force by then of a 57 mph wind. When at the highest point—an hour from home in good weather—the cloud came in thick, fast and wet. Crouching behind a high dyke that shook in the punching gusts I drank half a flask of hot honey-sweetened cocoa in preparation for the return and got soaked immediately. Later I was blown off course when hopping from clump to clump to avoid sinking into bog and couldn't see much further than a few yards ahead. Pushing into a 60 mph wind gusting to 70 was exhilarating but I'm glad, before leaving, that I ate porridge which gave me the burn. I was exhausted but dared not stop to crouch and shelter for more than a few moments because if I did so my sweat would quickly turn cold and my joints stiffen. I lit the fire before removing my wet clothes. Even though well-wrapped and sealed every item was saturated. A strong wind in an exposed situation finds ways to penetrate the most securely fastened and zipped-up clothing. I'd hardly slept the night before and was feeling raggy, buffeted and perhaps a little depressed by the tile-ripping, sleep-depriving storm.

In the last twenty-four hours of tidal winds more tiles were blown off, then gutters and a drainpipe, then eventually a chimney-pot. The house is coming apart from the roof down. Lying directly beneath it my ears pop from the pressure of the gusts, loose tiles rattle and the draught penetrates beneath the bed-covers. To survive in this exposed situation I have to 'engage' the weather, in both a strategic and Romantic sense. Enough of these drowsy ramblings and time to get up.

5TH JANUARY

Bright day, still. Sunrise and three or four layers of colour to the north and west. Mid-afternoon and the sky overcast except for a gash of low sun and a pale green light over snow-covered mountains and the wintry wastes of these hills in the foreground.

I went to bed at eight to economize on the coal as my account is overdrawn. The car is off the road, even if I could dig it out, for the same reason.

7TH JANUARY

A startling dawn draws a bright day. I took another stiff walk
and my balaclava became caked with frozen breath within min-
utes. There's a strong wind blowing from the north-east and a
Helm Bar forming over the Eden.

> The 'Helm Wind' to an observer on the south-western slope of
> the Crossfell escarpment is a strong and steady wind blowing
> directly down the slope. It appears to issue and probably de-
> rives its name from the characteristic 'helm' or mass of cloud
> which, viewed from the western flank of the Northern Pen-
> nines, extends uniformly along or just above the crest of the
> range with a thickness varying from a few hundred to several
> thousand feet on a majority of occasions when the prevailing
> wind across N. England is north-easterly.
>
> From the crest to the foot of the range the ground falls, in
> the neighbourhood of Crossfell, two thousand feet in about
> 2½ miles i.e., 1 in 6 overall. As long as the slope is not greater
> than 1:3 approximately, the air flows smoothly and steadily
> down the escarpment, but towards the summit where the lime-
> stone scars outcrop with very steep slopes it is possible to stand
> in their lee in relative calm while the strong flow of air can be

heard a few feet above. It is also noteworthy that this surface flow near the summit becomes more marked in the gullies; while, near the foot, complete shelter can be obtained under walls and in the lee of the belts of trees which have in the past been planted for this purpose. *

Helm Wind—a sack of fiends thrown in a vortex tear themselves to pieces.

---

*Gordon Manley, 'The Helm Wind of Crossfell 1937–1939', *Quarterly Journal of the Royal Meteorological Society* (July–October 1945): 201.

9TH JANUARY

Woke from a dream about coming home to find my then-lover packing her bags. As she walked up the street I threw open the window to shout.

When I did wake up and open the window to see what kind of day it was I disturbed two ravens, large and black against the snow.

White mist, a light wind; otherwise silent.

The door, which opens outward, is blocked by a snowdrift up to the gutter. Mist reflects snow and I can't tell where one begins or the other ends.

12TH JANUARY

A westerly brings freezing cloud and it's a whiteout. It's hard to keep warm; even when wearing several pair of thick socks my feet remain icy. The force of the gale is lifting the roof tiles a mere yard from my head as I work on Jamie Allan. My ears pop when the house, like the inside of a concertina, contracts and expands as the air is violently sucked in and then out.

CHAPTER VII

Allan assumes the Character of a Gentleman—Becomes a Gamester—Ruin—Sudden appearance of his Gypsy Wife—Travels to Dumfries—Arrest for Theft—Love in a Prison—Escape and Generosity—Suffering on the Road—Benevolent Female—Curious Feat at Carlisle—Arrival at Whitehaven—Meets with a Gypsy Queen—Induced to change his Route.

13TH JANUARY

The clouds were down, the wind raged like a dying bull but I managed to push through a four-mile walk—which seemed shorter in the fog—keeping below the wind where I could and behind tall dykes. I've been trying to think of a name for Jamie Allan's girlfriend—something of a foxy doxy.

Made soup with leeks, spuds, coriander, chilli (too many), carrots and celeriac. Drank the first glass of wine in a week, smoked a spliff and listened to Schubert's songs and string quartets. I find Scarlatti's sonatas better for working, as they were written as exercises, I'm told, and often demand fast-finger thinking—which suits my typing. Flamenco guitar also works perfectly for the purpose.

My first encounter with classical music was on the BBC Third Programme, exploring stations on the wireless when I was twelve or thirteen. Although we had a piano in the house my parents couldn't afford a teacher and it was never on offer at school, but every time the house was empty I would run ignorant fingers along the keys trying to find something in there. Roy Fisher's poem about a piano comes to mind:

To play is to go searching in the keyboard;
to make music's to recognize what's found.

I never did learn to play and regret the lack of a teacher to show me how. By the time I heard Jerry Lee Lewis and Little Richard rattling the ivories it was too late—no more piano, but I found a teacher of another kind, in Bunting.

THE SHORT-EARED OWL AS
GROUND-NESTING METAPHOR

Roy Fisher said
owl is low
spelt inside out.

L flaps to the front
and the W,
hatched
and flown back,
splays
like a tail
over O
rolled
and nestled

waiting
to
toowoo
again.

14TH JANUARY

It feels as though this westerly might rip off the roof and my lugs ache as it shakes the walls and the floor. There's no hiding from this weather so I wrapped and padded my ears, protected my face from the flesh-ripping gale and walked to Fiends Fell, which is the most exposed point for miles. As I stood with my back to the gale my trousers flapped furiously, slapping and tugging my legs, like anxious hungry tongues flicking, brushing and caressing the end of my cock in a kind of foreplay to a blow job. Perhaps that's why it was called Fiends Fell; although the North Pennines' highest hill, Cross Fell, reputedly bore the same name before Christian missionaries drove out the 'fiends' and renamed it.

16TH JANUARY

The bedroom was bitter cold when I woke and the wind mean. Mist driven over the fell fills the valley. Vortex above the wind-stripped hills riddled with overgrown workings, collapsed shafts, tools rusting into dust and abandoned mines.

There's a black heavy cloud driven over the escarpment and it hangs there, the edge of a blanket capping the peak, turning on a spit, withering away from its edges; unspun wool on a spindle.

Back to my bed of winds—a ship on a rough sea. I forgot what I was going to write. Sucked into a vortex.

We put our markers down—tracks in snow.

NECTARINE

I forgot forget
amnesia
was lost to me

then a smooth
fur-free fruit
unnamed for days

until I found it
ripe
on my tongue

19TH JANUARY

Mist forms in long gullies and the mountains beyond are blue, silvery gold and dove grey. Snow-ripples shadowed through drifts. Water over a fall blown back on its course.

> . . . *shuttles thrown*
> *like drops from a fountain, spray, mist of spiderlines*
> *bearing the rainbow . . .*
> —Bunting's *Briggflatts*

When I climbed down into Graining Beck, amongst the black wet boulders a peregrine flew out from the rock face and hugged the contours of this tight clough for about fifty yards until it reached a rowan tree growing out of the cliff and perched. It would have watched me scramble down the steep slopes to the water's edge where I found an explosion of recently plucked pigeon feathers.

The wind like a pack of feral dogs on the heels of a sheep. Quickly shifting moods.

As I walked along the beck and looked down on the remains of a barite mine abandoned in the 1940s by the few dozen men that would have worked it, the old Northumbrian song 'Sair Fyeld Hinny' came to mind and the occasion that I first heard it. I must have been about eighteen and there was a small gathering at our flat in Newcastle after a reading in the Morden Tower. Our baby son Matthew was asleep, a couple of friends had guitars and we were happy and high on drink and grass and each other's company. On those occasions, Basil might break into a saucy song by Marie Lloyd or another musical-hall favourite and sometimes 'Bollocky Bill the Sailor':

> 'Who's that knocking at my door?' said the fair Young
> Maiden.
> 'It's me and my crew and we've come for a screw!' said
> Bollocky Bill the Sailor.

But on this night, after a couple of deep pulls on the spliff going round, he became solemn and began to sing:

> Sair fyeld hinny, sair fyeld noo
> Sair fyeld hinny, sin' a' kenned thou

Aa was young and lusty aa was fair and clear
Aa was young and lusty many's a lang year

Sair fyeld hinny, sair fyeld noo
Sair fyeld hinny, sin' a kenned thou

When I was five and twenty aa could lowp a dyke
Noo am five and sixty aa can barely step a syke

Sair fyeld sair fyeld noo
Sair fyeld hinny, sin aa kenned thoo

Thus spoke the owld man to the old oak tree
Sair fyeld is aa sin' a kend thee!

He had a good voice and it lives with me overlooking the clough,
turning my face away from bitter winds into the gaze of an old
hawthorn, knarred and spiky, where I took shelter in a scooped-
out sheep-kip amongst its roots on the edge of a cliff and made
this note.

Sair fyeld hinny, sair fyeld noo
Sair fyeld hinny, sin aa kenned thoo

23RD JANUARY

Bright constellations and a half-moon's light reflected in the café's frosted roof tiles.

A fierce north-easterly lacerates flesh, spins a tango over a small freezing tarn on Fiends Fell, etching scribbles on ice. In an attempt to find a pattern of direction—to record or even paint the wind—I take pictures.

> *Reeds bent by rime.*
> *Movement in a still frames the invisible.*

3RD FEBRUARY

Blizzards for much of the day. Too cold to work in the attic bedroom and the living room never quite warm enough to read or write. The snow is powdery and paints the wind in a dervish dance.

The question occurs: is Saddam more dangerous to the world than an unfettered America?

As my water supply is pumped from a spring down the hill I'm worried it will cut out again so don't empty the bath but save it for flushing the toilet. A dental appointment had to be cancelled as I'm snowed up, and the car is buried. In an attempt to see daylight I went to clear the snow from my windows and it took a while and much effort to force the door open to dig my way through a drift that reached the roof. But I am tempted to wrap up and head down to Graining Beck if possible, as I failed to get out yesterday and as far as I remember did no work.

From the moment that I began this entry a clear view of the valley has collapsed into a few meters of fog. I'm so disorganized that it's difficult to sit and work solidly—often the only place to sit is on top of the pathetic fire.

Animals have scratched out patches of green in the snow. A bomber flies overhead, leaving vapor trails in the childhood blue.

snow echoes silence

rushes feather
a hoarfrost headdress

caretaker of sunsets
doorkeeper of dawn

the small sound of narrow waters
follow my tracks back

that's why I left them there

5TH FEBRUARY

Having slept without the radio to lull me out of insomniac thought and because there was no wind, I woke refreshed, with sunlight on the bed and a horn in my hand—conscious of solitude in a way that's new. There was a 30 mph wind and a taste of spring this morning but I'm unable to attribute that to the bright weather or the stiff cock.

I heard a golden plover—and saw, for the first time at this height, a solitary lapwing passing over and down into the shelter of the Eden Valley, where there are flocks. But up here, spring, when it does eventually arrive, comes cautiously, strung in wind, bringing snipes, curlews, pipits and a web of lark song.

clouds shift,
shiver out the sun

a slanting sheet of sleet
driven over the fells

from the east

a gust of sun
and some bird thinks it spring

the river in flood
in a misaligned season

although we burn in bed
we bicker above the beck

her breath expects
wind and river rip

8TH FEBRUARY

The weather here is overseer. Snow turns to rain. Light with-
draws; hill mists drift to lip Long Tongue. The woven day dimin-
ishes.

sleet storms veil the fells
flickers into snow

my pen scratches paper
flames crack

As I wrote by the window I followed sunlight across my desk as
though it were an errant blanket on a cold night.

rain rush on glass
a lump of coal shifts in the grate

My bronchial father—pale bony face and large brown eyes—
tickles the flame beneath a simmering kettle as my mother, who's
been charring on the other side of town, walks up the street and
into sight. Spuggies flutter in the gutter, a passing vehicle and his
wheezing lungs. *Help me take these booties off*, she said at the
threshold, the kettle steaming, *my feet are killing me*.

9TH FEBRUARY

night rides up long slopes
mist fills the valley

overlapping greys patch a hung-over sky

the faint curve of a distant brow
wind-wracked rains insist on glass

10TH FEBRUARY

The wind demands attention, whispers—silk slipped under consciousness—then strikes; a wild cat at the end of its tether.

The ground is frozen and a flock of crows skims in and out of the fog, close to the scrub and below the hem of the gale.

On the way to Long Tongue I climbed into a deep shake-hole where a syke licked over the rock edge to make a trickle of head-water music.

11TH FEBRUARY

a rabid dog on a long leash leaps,
howls lurching through power lines

lashing out fast and pugnacious,
a punch-drunk heavyweight on speed.

12TH FEBRUARY

Late at night, without a coat and the wind still raging, an old woman from the cottage hospital in Alston, banging on the deserted mortuary window, demanding entry—convinced she is home.

Water drapes over worn flattened rocks, smooth as curtains.

14TH FEBRUARY

Four in the afternoon: a wind-swirled sketch on a tarn's surface of calligraphic fish and fins feathered and winged as the water freezes. Clouds move slowly past as I drift around the pool until the sun blackens and engraved lines delineate.

After looking into frozen water and into thought I turned and fleetingly caught, behind a parting sky, the moon in alignment with the tarn and dripping sun, before clouds obscured again.

night blows up fast from the valley
dykes dissolve in thick fog
I follow my feet home

20TH FEBRUARY

By mid-afternoon I was chasing cage fever so wrapped myself in several layers of clothing—leaving no flesh exposed to a riving wind—threw on a back-pack and headed down Rickers Gill through patches of wet rushes and stubborn heather to the snow-line. As I descended the steep slippery banks of Graining Beck the stream ran fast below the old stone lime-kilns. There was sufficient thaw to swell the waters and I could hear the beck's busy echo long before seeing it. When I eased my way down, trying not to brush against clinging thistles, I slipped and instinctively grabbed at the earth to regain my balance and won a palm full of microscopic pricks in my pores.

Further upstream two precisely placed heron's footprints in the snow. The bird had taken the same route and wondering how long they'd been there I followed, until the prints ended after a few yards, amongst thin reeds at the quickening rush of the water's edge.

The stream twists and turns and loses height suddenly so that many pools form and banks sheer without footing but sometimes, as it momentarily flattens and meanders, there is a choice of banks to walk. I chose the east with its slightly steeper grassy slope instead of the west with a flattened track through slippery shale. This is the choice I make every time, I thought, jumping from rock to rock across the stream and catching sight of the heron's imprint opposite. It too had taken this route so I followed its tracks as the light dimmed.

a heron
criss-crosses the lashing syke,
fast with sudden thaw,

its spiky tread sunk
in unscuffed snow

patient
and hungry as death

no inkling of urgency
in its measured step

close, almost overlapping,
at the water's edge

The day had been cloudy mostly. It was now 3.30 pm, fifteen minutes from sunset, and a stiff and potentially hazardous climb to safe footing before the night overtook.

As I approached the tight and sudden confluence of three streams, a half-moon slightly brightened the dark sky above the narrows. A heron flew past painting air with its primaries, retracing its tracks and mine. With only the lunar half-light to find my footing up the narrow clough I stepped across rocks to higher ground until I reached the ziggurat-like track, winding up from the remains of a deserted barite mine, which was my way out of there. A low jet roared overhead rehearsing a raid on Iraq.

> *May the sacred river Ulay mourn you,*
>   *along whose banks we walked in our vigour!*
> *May the pure Euphrates mourn you,*
>   *whose water we poured in libation from skins!*
>
> *May the young men of Uruk-the-Sheepfold mourn you,*
>   *who saw us slay the Bull of Heaven!*
> *May the ploughman mourn you in his furrows*
>   *when he sows your name in song* *

---

*The Epic of Gilamesh, adapted from a translation by Andrew George.

When I climbed up to the edge of the fell I took a step into myself and found a predatory instinct. A sneaping wind was blowing around the top of the 'ziggurat' and to stay out of its icy bite for as long as possible I descended again into the deep shadows of the narrow clough to a sheep track level with the stream which would provide shelter up the steep wind-ripped hill to the damp patch of its source where I would become exposed for the final mile home to the unfettered, unhindered and unhinged gale.

LARK & MERLIN

1

a wren,
perched on a hawthorn
low enough to skip
the scalping winds,

sang a scalpel song

.

sea frets drift
sheer along shorelines

in a café without customers,
listening to hail spray glass,
and wind and a waitress laugh,
I fell to fell thinking

a sullen light through vapour
thins a line of hills

the edge of everything is nothing
whipped by wind

watched on a webcam
bound to a bedpost
gag on my shaft

rose blush of roadkill rabbit
insides out on Tarmacadam

cumulus in a tarn
its fast shadow
flees far hills

a wave of sleek grass
skiffs mist

my hand thought of her
a photograph
waiting to happen

this come-to-kill wind
rips at the root

here she comes
and there she goes
rushes bow to rime

I should shut down
close off
stop

if I could

how quick the mist
how quick

2

my lover, the assassin,
is beautiful

she has come to kill me
and I concur

just now she sleeps
but when she wakes I'm dead

her eyelids flitter
as I prepare her potions,
her delicious poisons

as she flew past a lick
of her melodic nectar
stuck to my wing,
making flight, for an instant,
sticky

but nothing preening couldn't fix

she asked about my heart,
its evasive flight;
but can I trust her with its secrets?

and does the merlin, in fast pursuit of its prey,
tell the fleeing lark it is enamoured of its song?

or the singing lark turn tail
and fly into the falcon's talons?

my heart, the cartographer, charts
to the waterline,
is swept back as the tide turns
wiping the map blank, wave
after moon-drawn wave

walking home I stride these tracks
with her tread

3

it has gone on for days

strumming rushes
taking up tales,
taking them on
the fall of my foot, on tufts

a stroke of light along a law lain in under a long cloud

I accrete—lichen to limestone
sphagnum to peat

late shadows gather in the dark

words unwrite
as they are written
unspeak
as they are spoken

songs sprung
from heart and lung
to tongue

unsung

drunk winds
stumble over shuffling roofs
shake his sleep who dreams
a lost love
will not
let
go

recurring swirls
of old gold
blown light

you can't help
but be in it

as it opens
and falls back on itself
unfolds and unsays

I do not want to die
without writing the unwritten

pleasure of water